THE IMPORTER'S

───── JACK BUTLER ─────

THE IMPORTER'S HANDBOOK

A practical guide to successful importing

Woodhead-Faulkner

NEW YORK   LONDON   TORONTO   SYDNEY   TOKYO

First published 1988 by
Woodhead-Faulkner (Publishers) Limited
Campus 400, Maylands Avenue
Hemel Hempstead
Hertfordshire, HP2 7EZ

A division of
Simon & Schuster International Group

© Jack Butler 1988

All rights reserved. No part of this publication may be reproduced, stored in a retrieval system, or transmitted, in any form, or by any means, electronic, mechanical, photocopying, recording or otherwise, without prior permission, in writing, from the publisher.

Typeset by Pentacor Ltd, High Wycombe, Bucks.
Printed and bound in Great Britain by
Antony Rowe Ltd, Chippenham, Wiltshire

British Library Cataloguing in Publication Data

A catalogue record for this book is available from
the British Library

ISBN 0-85941-310-1 (pbk)

2 3 4 5   97 96 95 94 93

To my dearly loved late wife
PATRICIA
who, during the writing of this book,
was at once both my constant source of
encouragement and support
and my most demanding critic.

CONTENTS

Part One – The Background to International Trade

1. **Introduction** — 3
   - *1.1 A brief history of international trade* — 3
     - 1.1.1 The economics of international trade — 3
     - 1.1.2 The origins of international trade — 5
     - 1.1.3 Britain's role in international trade — 6
   - *1.2 The post-war years* — 8
     - 1.2.1 The oil crisis of 1973 — 8
     - 1.2.2 The oil crisis of 1978 — 11
     - 1.2.3 North Sea oil — 12
     - 1.2.4 The General Agreement on Tariffs and Trade (GATT) — 13
     - 1.2.5 The European Economic Community — 15

2. **Government trade departments** — 20
   - *2.1 The structure of government* — 20
   - *2.2 HM Customs and Excise* — 21
     - 2.2.1 History — 21
     - 2.2.2 Structure and functions — 22
   - *2.3 The Department of Trade and Industry* — 22
     - 2.3.1 History — 22
     - 2.3.2 Structure and functions — 23

3. **The structure of international trade** — 25
   - *3.1 The classification of trading nations* — 25
     - 3.1.1 The state trading system — 25
     - 3.1.2 The open market system — 26
     - 3.1.3 Formal open market groupings — 28
     - 3.1.4 The Organisation for Economic Co-operation and Development (OECD) — 29

	3.1.5 The ex-colonial networks	31
	3.1.6 Generalised schemes of preference	31
3.2	*The EEC special relationship network*	32
	3.2.1 Association agreements	32
	3.2.2 The Lomé Convention	32
	3.2.3 The EEC's generalised scheme of preferences	33
3.3	*Patterns of international trade*	34
	3.3.1 Trade flows in the international market	34
	3.3.2 The structure of UK trade	35
3.4	*Special forms of trade*	38
	3.4.1 Entrepot trading	38
	3.4.2 Outward and inward processing relief	39
	3.4.3 Countertrade	41
3.5	*Channels of trade*	42
	3.5.1 Direct importing - foreign manufacturer to distributor	42
	3.5.2 The role of agencies and other import specialists	43
	3.5.3 Free trade zones	45

4. The regulation of international trade — 48

4.1	*The instruments of regulation*	48
	4.1.1 Customs and Excise charges	48
	4.1.2 Quotas	49
	4.1.3 Currency controls	50
	4.1.4 Government subsidies	51
	4.1.5 Non-tariff barriers to trade	51
4.2	*The functions of the General Agreement on Tariffs and Trade*	52
	4.2.1 The most favoured nation principle (MFN)	52
	4.2.2 Anti-dumping procedures	53
	4.2.3 Derogations from the general principles	53
	4.2.4 Voluntary restraint agreements (VRAs)	54
	4.2.5 The Multi-Fibre Arrangement (MFA)	55
4.3	*Special EEC provisions*	61
	4.3.1 Free circulation	61
	4.3.2 The role of harmonisation	64
	4.3.3 Competition policy	65
	4.3.4 The Common Agricultural Policy (CAP)	67

Part Two – The Practice of Importing

5. **The import transaction** 73
   - 5.1 *Transaction preliminaries* 73
     - 5.1.1 Types and stages of transactions 73
     - 5.1.2 The order 74
     - 5.1.3 Terms and conditions 77
     - 5.1.4 Settlement terms and payments 78
   - 5.2 *Miscellaneous issues* 80
     - 5.2.1 Samples 80
     - 5.2.2 Aftersales servicing arrangements 81
     - 5.2.3 Product pricing 83
     - 5.2.4 Requirements of exporting countries 85
     - 5.2.5 Health, safety, and consumer protection 86
     - 5.2.6 Trading Standards officers 88

6. **Import entry procedures** 89
   - 6.1 *HM Customs legal instruments* 89
     - 6.1.1 Customs legal requirements 89
     - 6.1.2 The import licence 90
     - 6.1.3 *The Tariff* 91
   - 6.2 *Customs 88* 94
     - 6.2.1 General introduction 94
     - 6.2.2 The Harmonised Commodity Description and Coding System (HS) 94
     - 6.2.3 The Integrated Customs Tariff (TARIC) 96
     - 6.2.4 The Single Administrative Document (SAD) 97
     - 6.2.5 The Customs handling of import and export freight (CHIEF) 100
     - 6.2.6 The importer and the introduction of Customs 88 101
   - 6.3 *Transportation and insurance* 103
     - 6.3.1 Freight handling and transportation 103
     - 6.3.2 Risks and insurance 109
     - 6.3.3 Taking delivery of goods from the carrier 114
   - 6.4 *Entry procedures and documentation* 115
     - 6.4.1 Customs procedures in general 115
     - 6.4.2 State trading nations procedures 118
     - 6.4.3 The EEC preference schemes procedures 119

	6.4.4 Multi Fibre Arrangement procedures	120
	6.4.5 Common Agricultural Policy procedures	121
	6.4.6 Outward and inward processing relief	123
	6.4.7 Free trade zones procedures	124
	6.4.8 Rules of origin	125
	6.4.9 Customs valuation	126
	6.4.10 Suspension of duty	129
	6.4.11 Trade statistics	129
7	**Import finance**	**131**
	7.1 Payments to be made	131
	7.1.1 Customs duty and excise	131
	7.1.2 Value added tax	131
	7.2 Methods of financing imports	132
	7.2.1 Loans, guarantees and discounts	132
	7.2.2 Currency arrangements	134
8.	**New technology and international trade**	**136**
9.	**Sources of information and assistance**	**138**
	9.1 Institutional facilities	138
	9.2 Useful publications	140
	Appendix A The terms of trade	141
	Appendix B Inland clearance centres	143
	Appendix C The Integrated Tariff of the United Kingdom – specimen page	145
	Appendix D The Single Administrative Document (C88) – specimen form	147
	Appendix E List of forms replaced by the SAD (C88)	149
	Appendix F The international trading affiliation network	151
Index		**157**

PREFACE

First, I have to acknowledge that I owe the idea for this book to the publishers, Woodhead-Faulkner, who first noticed the almost complete absence of a general, consolidated guide to the importation of goods into the United Kingdom.

For the exporter, there is a bewildering embarrassment of riches in terms of advice, but, for the importer, little at all. Yet the British economy, and in particular the British consumer, depends as much on the entrepreneurial skills of importers as of exporters, British industry depends on imports of raw materials and components, and consumers depend on competitively priced food and other consumable goods from other countries for a progressive, low inflationary improvement in their standard of living.

The time, too, is particularly appropriate in that widespread changes in the classification, administration and documentation of imports were introduced, on 1 January 1988, under the general title 'Customs 88'. These changes are designed primarily to widen the application of new technologies to trading practices throughout the world and thus to improve the speed and efficiency of international trading.

In Britain, we are fortunate that HM Customs and Excise does not see itself as the first natural barrier between consumers and their needs. They are genuinely anxious to maintain the flow of foreign trade in both directions and to reduce the delays generated by the labyrinth of constraints imposed on it by the various regimes and treaties which have been concluded over the years.

This book is divided into two parts. The objective of Part One is to provide a wide, general background to world trade – its history, its practices and the complicated network of relationships which has evolved in order to expand and control it. The objective of Part Two is to provide a general description of the practices of importing goods into the United Kingdom, with particular reference to the changes in documentary procedures made under 'Customs 88'.

In writing Part Two, I have been particularly aware of the necessity to avoid detailed descriptions of current procedures and practices because they are in a constant state of change and amendment. Any book which attempts to describe them without providing a comprehensive up-dating service becomes out of date almost before the printer's ink is dry. Instead, therefore, I have provided a brief description of the scope of and intent behind the various procedures, practices and documentation and then cross-referenced them to the relevant customs notices or sections of HM Customs publication, *The Integrated Tariff of the United Kingdom*. These notices are being constantly altered, yet retain their original reference numbers so that the reader of this book can, by obtaining the latest version of each notice, be sure that he has the latest direction and advice on that particular subject.

World trade, when seen in the round, is a complex and daunting subject because, in writing about it, it is necessary to encompass all produce groups imported from all sources. In practice, of course, individual traders tend to specialise both in products and in their sourcing and, when this occurs, the procedures become, if not simpler, then at least more familiar to the user. In this book, I advocate the practice of developing a custom-built 'in-house' instruction manual designed to cover the procedures and documentation of the specific goods and sources which each trader imports.

The final objective of the book is brevity. I have tried to cover the ground in the fewest possible words, because practising importers are busy people and any time spent on reading can always be better employed in making money. The book is therefore what is often described as 'close-textured' which can all too readily be a different way of saying 'unreadable'. I can only hope that, in this case, clarity has not been sacrificed on the altar of brevity.

The book is intended to do the following:

1. To serve as a short guide for practising importers to the voluminous literature provided by HM Customs and Excise and to the 'up-date' reference services such as Croners.
2. To provide a general background description of world trade for those who directly or indirectly manage import activities.
3. To introduce import history and practices to those who intend to make a career in commerce which might involve importing in one form or another.
4. To be used as a first reader or textbook on importing for business management studies at all levels.
5. To act as a reference facility in academic, business and public libraries.

In writing this book, I have been forced to rely heavily on the knowledge and experience of others and would take this opportunity to thank most sincerely Graham Smith of HM Customs and Excise, (whose own book, *Something to Declare*, concerning the history of his service I found so engrossing that it put back my writing schedule by over a fortnight). Keith Robinson and his colleagues at the Merseyside Chamber of Commerce, Bob Anderson, who heads the DTI team in the Merseyside Task Force, Roger Coates, Roy Skelton and Emma Ormond of the British Importers Confederation (and Roger in particular for preserving me from the worst of many factual errors in the original draft), Frank Robotham, of the Liverpool Freeport and Michael Corrigan, Sefton MBC's Principal Trading Standards Officer. In particular, I would thank Alan Richardson, long-standing friend and Secretary of the Southport Chamber of Commerce, for his patient reading of the manuscript as it evolved and his insistence that he at least understood what I was trying to say. I also must thank John Reeves and his students at ITEC, a very successful Southport Youth Training Scheme, for their assistance in word-processing the final version of the manuscript after I had clumsily lost a large chunk of it when trying to be too clever on my own machine.

Jack Butler

PART ONE

THE BACKGROUND TO INTERNATIONAL TRADE

1

INTRODUCTION

1.1 A BRIEF HISTORY OF INTERNATIONAL TRADE

1.1.1 The economics of international trade

Economists, as usual, have a theory about international trade. They call it the 'law of comparative costs'. This 'law' seeks to explain why, if one country has a certain competitive advantage over others in terms of either natural resources or production costs, then specialisation in that product is of benefit to all and international trade will result.

One-way trade in the product will be generated, regardless of whether the receiving country can offer reciprocal advantages in other products. This is why Japan and Germany are able to sustain substantial positive balances in their visible trade and the United States of America even larger deficits over quite long periods. Misbalances in trade in goods, that is to say 'visible' trade, are compensated for by a variety of other economic and financial activities. Britain, for example, runs a persistent deficit on its visible non-oil account, yet manages to achieve healthy surpluses in its overall balance of payments for most of the time by trading in services such as insurance and international banking, otherwise known as 'invisibles'. If, of course, the deficit in a country's balance of payments persists, then its government may have to introduce fiscal and economic controls, usually with serious political consequences (like losing the next election), but this is another story altogether.

The law of comparative costs also holds good for regional advantages within national economies, but in international trade other factors tend to intervene:

1. As national identity develops, national differences in law, language, tax regimes, life styles and political structures emerge.
2. Each country evolves its unique monetary system and seeks to control and manipulate its currency to its best advantage.
3. Most countries feel the need to becomes as self-sufficient as possible:

therefore they protect their strategic agricultural and industrial bases with trade and other barriers.
4. Although each country exerts direct control over its own economy, it has no direct control over the policies of others, and these policies may affect its well-being. Therefore nearly all countries seek to use trade as a diplomatic and political negotiating weapon.
5. Countries with different lifestyles, tastes, standards of living and attitudes to safety and quality often find it difficult to assimilate unfamiliar products from other countries however useful or attractive they may be in terms of price and value.
6. There is often a deep-rooted feeling of distrust and even disloyalty about buying foreign goods.

The international trading scene is bedevilled by these conflicts of interest, real or imagined. So those who wish to enter the field have to overcome these barriers by demonstrating and marketing clear competitive advantages to the consumers and industrialists with whom they are attempting to trade.

Any country wishing to control the flow of its trade needs mechanisms for doing so and these mechanisms take five basic forms:

1. Tariffs and duties.
2. Quotas.
3. Currency controls.
4. Subsidies.
5. Non-tariff barriers.

A further economic complication is what is known as the 'terms of trade'. For example, between World Wars I and II, as a result of technical improvements in agriculture, there was a worldwide over-production of basic foodstuffs. Consequently, it cost Britain substantially less to import her food needs than before and thus she required less exports to cover the cost of them (which was just as well, because they were falling rapidly anyway). So, as the terms of trade change, there can be significant changes in the balance of payments, even if little or no change occurs in the volume of trade. This can frequently conceal for a time real structural weaknesses in a country's trading position.

The nineteenth century brought an intensive analysis of world trade. The majority of the great political economists – Adam Smith, Ricardo, Hume and Mill – advocated free trade as opposed to the then widely-practised doctrine of 'mercantilism', a term which covered all the devices for the control of trade and the protection of domestic industries and interests which had been developing since the Middle Ages. The theory of the free traders can be simply stated:

1. Protection favours producers not consumers.
2. Free trade lowers prices.
3. Loss of economic independence lowers the risk of war.

However, these theories make light of some very real problems which national governments have to face:

1. The need to protect their domestic industries.
2. The need to maintain a national skills base.
3. The need to prevent regional unemployment in traditional industries caused by cheap imports.
4. The need to protect domestic industries against dumping at uneconomic prices.

Much intellectual effort and not a little ink has been wasted on the 'free trade v. mercantilism' debate, for few of the protagonists have been prepared to accept that the pragmatic solution lies in achieving a proper balance between the two and the real argument is about the ingredients of the mix.

The result of all this theory and practice has been the emergence of a labyrinth of international treaties, agreements, arrangements and unilateral regulations which govern, promote and restrict the free flow of international trade. It is to the practical day-to-day operation of these restraints which this book addresses itself.

1.1.2 The origins of international trade

In the early Middle Ages, societies tended to be self-sufficient and national identities were weak. What today passes for international trade was conducted predominantly in lightweight luxury goods which were moved slowly along the great maritime, river and overland arteries of trade. In the Mediterranean basin, trade over the network of maritime coastal routes was dominated by the Greeks and Phoenicians. Inland, goods were carried by pack animals. Journeymen travelled the 'Great Loop' – Venice, Lombardy, Champagne, Flanders, Russia, Venice, – dropping off raw materials, collecting goods made up from them and trading at the great fairs and trade route intersections. Minor routes criss-crossed within the loop and where they crossed townships grew and thrived.

In the East, the main trade artery was the Great Silk Route. It started from Damascus and ran through Baghdad, Masahrad, Bokhara, Samarkand, Alma Ata and Langtou to finish some 5,000 miles away in the spice and silk markets of China. The caravans which travelled this route were in effect small mobile townships, self-sufficient in most domestic needs and services, which moved painfully slowly, stopping to trade at each point where the trade routes from Central Russia cross to India and beyond. Such a caravan might take five or six years to complete the round journey. The origins of custom duties lie in the tribute and taxes which the caravans were forced to pay to the nomads and overlords through whose territory they passed. The two major trading networks – Europe and the East – were linked by the entrepreneurial activities of the Venetian Republic, exploiting the relationships built up during the Crusades.

In the fourteenth century, Spain and Portugal, on the western fringe of the Mediterranean/Far Eastern trading network, were growing in wealth and confidence as ocean-going powers, a confidence reinforced by their religious support from and to the Vatican. Each sought to bypass the great overland routes to make themselves independent of Venice and its trading partners by discovering alternative sea routes to the same markets. In the process they accidentally discovered America. Once the imagination of Europeans was fired by the exploits of the Great Iberian navigators, they were quick to realise the potential for plunder revealed by their discoveries and interest in ocean trading quickened.

In the fifteenth centry, to avoid conflict and anarchy, the Vatican, still not quite certain that the earth was round, divided up the new worlds revealed by the navigators, by drawing a line down the middle of the Atlantic and awarding the western concession to Spain and the eastern concession to Portugal. The basis of this two-way trade can best be described as 'treasure in, religion out'.

It was during this time, also, that the sophisticated banking network which contributed so much to the expansion and safety of trade was developed. It had its origins in the Lombard towns of northern Italy. The framework and practices established by these pioneer bankers still form the basis of modern international commercial banking.

1.1.3 Britain's role in international trade

Today, Britain is among the least self-sufficient countries in the trading world, as she imports about 30 per cent of the goods she consumes or uses in her industrial processes. Throughout the nineteenth century, Britain led the world into industrialisation, which brought the following in its train:

1. A rapid decline in her self-sufficiency.
2. A concentration of increasingly wealthy wage-earners into urban conurbations.
3. An appetite for still larger foreign markets.
4. Improved and faster facilities for bulk transportation.
5. A rapid development of invisible trade.

Invisible trade is the jargon used to describe revenue-producing support services for trade in tangible (i.e. visible) goods (see section 3.4.4). From the 1850s, her insatiable appetite for industrial raw materials and, increasingly, cheap imported cereals, sugar and meat, led Britain into a substantial deficit on her visible trade account, but this was more than balanced by her invisible earnings. She was the first, but by no means the last, country to experience this phenomenon. The visible trade deficit was aggravated by increasing competition from Germany and the United States of America who were industrialising rapidly and who dominated the newer electrical and chemical industries. Both developed their industries from behind high tariff barriers.

Britain relied increasingly for the bulk of her export trade on coal, cotton, machinery and capital goods, such as railway rolling stock, and sought to encourage worldwide free trade. Two world wars did little to help. In the first of them, the United States of America became the self-styled 'arsenal of democracy' for the Allies and, in the process, built a modern, technology-based industrial structure which its multinational enterprises were able to exploit rapidly when peace returned.

After World War I, trade expanded significantly but Britain found that it had to share its markets not only with the United States but also with the expanding industries of other countries such as Japan. It also became necessary to accommodate two new major industrial sectors – automobiles and oil. Coal, which before 1914 had been a major contributor to the British export trade, was rapidly replaced by oil as the main source of mobile energy. Britain's other main export, cotton textiles, was coming increasingly under challenge from the low-cost mills of India and the Far East. Instead of responding to these changes, Britain sought, by government subsidy and other protectionist measures, to maintain its share of trade in its traditional sectors of coal, cotton textiles, steel and shipbuilding. Already however, industrial development in other countries was creating disastrous surpluses in these sectors and at the same time the markets for these products were contracting.

With the onset of the depression of the 1930s, Britain, in common with other mature industrialised countries, erected protectionist tariff barriers and propped up its agriculture with heavy subsidies. It also, in the face of growing competition from the United States, Europe and Japan, retreated behind the Empire Preference Scheme to the tied and relatively unsophisticated markets of its colonies and dominions. By 1938, 50 per cent of its trade was with these markets.

Although World War II was the major factor in curing the high unemployment created by the depression of the 1930s, it changed even more profoundly the pattern and distribution of world trade.

1. Air transport progressively challenged shipping as the most effective means of moving first, passengers and later, freight, about the world.
2. The American multinationals had remembered the lessons of World War I and set out, behind their war industries, to dominate world markets in oil, automobiles and aircraft as much through their marketing and distribution knowhow as through their competitive advantage of production scale.
3. Underdeveloped countries, including the newly-independent colonies of the fast-vanishing empires of Britain, France, Belgium and Holland, were determined, through industrialisation, to join the 'rich nations club' as rapidly as possible, and were supported in these ambitions by the availability of grant aid from the industrialised countries. As with Britain in the eighteenth century and the United States and Europe in the nineteenth, they sought to build up their industrial bases from behind a wall of protection, at the same time calling vociferously for open access to the markets of their benefactors.
4. The war-devastated industries of Western Germany and Japan revived rapidly and with a more or less clean slate, sought to dominate the sunrise markets such as electronics, computers, leisure goods and household appliances, telecommunications and biotechnology which for one reason or another Britain was disinclined to enter.

By the 1950s, under these compound pressures, markets for Britain's industrial products were either declining rapidly or heavily protected. World trade became in effect a bitter political struggle for the international distribution of added values and employment opportunities in face of overproduction on a worldwide scale. Worst of all perhaps, during the two world wars, Britain had been forced to sell a substantial proportion of her overseas investments to the United States of America to pay for war materials and supplies. So, after 1947, she had to learn somehow to earn her way without the benefits of large invisible earnings from these former overseas investments. It had become a very different world.

1.2 THE POST-WAR YEARS

After 1945, three main factors altered profoundly the pattern of world trade in general and Britain's trading role in particular – the oil situation, the General Agreement on Tariffs and Trade (GATT) and the European Economic Community (EEC).

1.2.1 The oil crisis of 1973

Between the wars and until the 1970s the prosperity of the Western democracies had been built largely on very cheap oil from the Middle East.

By 1973, the trade in oil, and in particular Middle East oil, was dominated and controlled by what are popularly known in the oil industry as the 'Seven Sisters' – seven multinational organisations, one British, one Anglo-Dutch, five American. Between them they owned the concessions on all the Middle East oilfields besides the necessary refining capacity, distribution networks and marketing resources to exploit their output.

In October 1973, the official posted price was fixed at $3 a barrel. The posted price is the price offered by the 'Sisters' for long-term contracts to their major customers. It was on this posted price that the oil companies paid their 50 per cent taxes to their Middle Eastern source governments. However, there was a glut of oil on the market and the oil companies were forced to grant widespread discounts to their customers.

The 'Seven Sisters' negotiated future prices annually with the Organisation of Petroleum Exporting Countries (OPEC). This organisation was formed in 1960 by Saudi Arabia, Iraq, Kuwait, Venezuela and Iran. Today, there are 13 members:

Algeria	Iran	Libya	Saudi Arabia
Ecuador	Iraq	Nigeria	United Arab Emirates
Gabon	Kuwait	Qatar	Venezuela
Indonesia			

The older members wished to conserve what they saw as a wasting asset by leaving as much oil as possible in the ground. However, a number of the new members, such as Algeria and Nigeria, with large development ambitions, were in favour of maximising immediate revenues. As a result of these differences, OPEC had become a negotiating force which the 'Sisters' were coming increasingly to ignore.

At the time of the meeting between the 'Sisters' and OPEC in October 1973, although there was still a confusion of objectives among OPEC members, they were becoming increasingly aware of the potential of oil as a diplomatic and political weapon and most were prepared to force through a doubling of the price from $3 to $6 a barrel, if necessary by cutting back on production. At the meeting, the refusal by the 'Sisters' to accept this increase set in motion a series of manoeuvres which were to transform forever the economies of the Western democracies and the pattern of world trade.

Their proposals rejected, OPEC members proceeded to implement both the cutback in production, as well as an absolute embargo on deliveries to any country giving material aid to Israel. Shortages were immediate and potentially devastating. By December 1973, prices on the Rotterdam spot market (always a volatile place because relatively marginal quantities of oil were traded to meet immediate shortfalls or to lay off short-term surpluses) had been raised to between $17 and $22 a barrel. By the time the embargo on countries offering aid to Israel was lifted in 1974, not only OPEC members but also their customers appreciated fully for the first time how potent a weapon oil had become. Trade in oil was now four times greater in value than trade in any other single product.

Another important effect of the oil price explosion was the transfer of vast amounts of wealth from the Western consuming countries to two classes of OPEC members:

1. The less-developed countries with new oil revenues such as Algeria, Mexico and Nigeria, who already had plans to spend as much of their revenues as they could lay their hands on, mostly with the Western industrialised countries.
2. The sparsely-populated, partriarchal Arab states, who also had their ambitious spending plans, but who could not possibly spend all their revenues as fast as they were now being generated.

Even the spending plans of the first of these classes took time to work through into contracts for the industries of the Western democracies. Consequently, in the early stages of the 1973 crisis, money was being converted from spending into savings on a vast global scale. The more that had to be spent on oil, the less there was to spend on other goods. With a slowdown in demand for these other goods and a withdrawal of money from the spending cycle, the world moved rapidly into a demand-led recession, which severely affected both the manufacturing exports of the Western industrialised countries and the standards of living in the less-developed non-oil countries.

Soon however, the OPEC development contracts started to flow through and the saving Gulf states soon began to learn the lesson that idle money is a useless commodity unless put to work. Putting it to work meant handing it over to Western bankers to recycle into the world's economic system in the form of petrodollar loans (because oil was traditionally traded in dollars). Western bankers accepted the challenge with more enthusiasm than discretion and could hardly believe their luck when they found that, because of the Koranic prohibition on usury, it was also cheap money to borrow. This did not prevent their lending it on at current high market rates with few questions asked.

By 1975, the world's trading system had adjusted itself to a posted oil price of around $12 a barrel, the OPEC countries were now placing development contracts and everybody began to realise that it was only the ownership of money which had changed, not the way in which the benefits from using it were distributed.

However the increase in oil prices had made it profitable to exploit oil deposits which, at $3 a barrel, had not previously been viable. The substantial reserves in Mexico, Alaska and the North Sea were now developed rapidly by companies which had no interest in joining the OPEC cartel. Another oil glut was in prospect, so the 'Seven Sisters' sat back to wait confidently for OPEC to fall apart.

1.2.2. The oil crisis of 1978

In 1978 the Shah of Iran was deposed and oil production in that country, the second largest in the world, ceased abruptly. Oil was again in short supply and panic at once set in; by the spring of 1979 the price on the volatile Rotterdam spot market had risen to $37 a barrel – ten times its price before the 1973 crisis – and many members of OPEC were determined that this should be reflected on the posted price on which their royalties were based. However, by this time, Saudi Arabia and some of the other older Gulf oil producers were having second thoughts. They now had so much money invested around the world through Western bankers that they readily appreciated the danger of destabilising it. So they persuaded their colleagues in OPEC to settle the posted price at around $27.50 a barrel and raised their output to ensure that this price was maintained.

The major sufferers were the less-developed non-oil countries who were again being squeezed two ways. They had to pay even more for their oil and were forced to reduce their purchases of other products accordingly. Also, with a return to recession, prices of the raw materials, on which they depended for their foreign currency needs, were falling. At the same time, the developed countries found that the higher oil prices were fuelling their industrial costs and these fed through into rising inflation. Suddenly, too, bankers found that they had been lending-on their clients' petrodollars at high risk; many borrowers were now unable to meet their obligations and, as more and more loans became due for repayment, the banks were being forced to reschedule them to avoid both themselves and their borrowers going bankrupt. Even today, technically, without these rescheduling activities many banks would be insolvent.

OPEC, with the new non-member producers in Alaska, Mexico and Britain anxious to recover their investment from oil sales as fast as possible, found themselves unable to balance supply with demand as they had formerly been able to do by manipulating their extraction rates. For some years the posted price settled at around $20–25 a barrel. Occasionally the Rotterdam spot market went mad and bit somebody but, inevitably, 1986 saw another oil glut which promised this time to be a chronic one. The price went spiralling down below the $10 mark and suddenly the newer high-cost fields began to lose their viability. The new producers found too that, if you chop off your nose, something rather nasty seems to happen to your face.

In 1987, at the time of writing, attempts are being made, with some success to match extraction rates to demand so as to stabilise the posted price at around $15–20 a barrel.

1.2.3 North Sea oil

It was against this background that the exploitation of oil in the North Sea began. In 1959, natural gas was found and exploited off the Dutch coast, but it was not until 1969 that significant deposits of oil were located in the Forth field off Aberdeen. Britain was anxious to make herself independent of Middle East oil but, with oil selling at around $3 a barrel, extraction from deep offshore sites was not commercially attractive. To achieve its objectives therefore, the British government granted exploitation rights (and with them most of the financial benefits) to the Seven Sisters – 35 per cent to BP and Shell and the remainder to the American companies. As a result, by the 1980s Britain was a major oil producer on the scale of Kuwait.

Although little benefit in terms of tax revenues accrued to the British government, the impact of the North Sea oil on Britain's trading pattern was far ranging. To illustrate this, in 1985, Britain had an overall surplus on her balance of trade of £3.5 billion. Without the contribution from oil of £8.8 billion and invisible trade of £5.7 billion, she would have had an overall trade deficit of £10.8 billion overall. The balance of £8.8 billion in oil was made up of exports of £13 billion balanced by imports of £4.2 billion. Britain could not become self-sufficient in oil in the sense that the North Sea production replaced Gulf oil directly, because North Sea oil was of low tar content (which attracts a price premium). British refining capacity was in the main designed to cope with the high-tar oils of the Gulf. She therefore exported her higher price oil and bought in lower-grade Gulf oil at a net gain both in terms of price per barrel and of total revenues.

By the mid-1980s, North Sea oil had transformed Britain's balance of payments and currency reserves, and had largely repaired the damage wrought to her overseas investments by the two world wars. On the debit side, it has probably damaged irreparably British manufacturing industry: in the early 1980s, Britain became a net importer of manufactured goods for the first time in her history and has remained so ever since. In doing so, she had also contributed more than a little to her high rate of unemployment. Today, Britain is perceived by the world's financial markets to be a petro-economy, with her future prosperity tied to the price of oil. This is of course nonsense, as oil contributes only some 7 per cent to the country's GNP, but that is how the world perceives her and reacts to its perceptions.

As things stand today, the balance of Britain's economy is very vulnerable to low oil prices. A barrel of Gulf oil can still be brought to the surface for cents only, whereas the same amount of oil can cost $11 to lift from the

North Sea. A price level which was sustained for any length of time below, say $15 a barrel makes the development of new fields only marginally viable, if at all. Unfortunately also, North Sea oil as a natural resource, (in contrast to the Middle East with its vast reserves), is a fast-wasting asset. Already oil's contribution to the economy is past its peak. Well before the twenty-first century Britain will again be almost wholly dependent on imported oil.

1.2.4 The General Agreement on Tariffs and Trade (GATT)

After the Second World War, there was a general determination not to allow world trade to relapse back into the protectionist practices which were so rife and so damaging between the wars. In 1948, 23 nations signed the General Agreement on Tariffs and Trade. Since then, the GATT has become the forum for successive rounds of trade liberalisation and the guardian of the rules agreed by its signatories for the conduct of world trade. Britain was a founder member of this group. Today there are 92 members, two-thirds of them developing countries: the notable absentees are China, the Soviet Union and the remainder of the Comecon countries.

As a starting point, the GATT accepted that it would be quite unreasonable to expect sovereign states to stand by and see their economies and employment eroded by unrestricted imports. Therefore the individual packages of protection which each country had devised to meet its own special needs should remain for the time being as there was no practicable possibility of finding a common set of trading rules which all could adopt. Instead, it was agreed to allow the then existent patterns of protection to stand and seek to reduce and dismantle them gradually and progressively. The doctrine adopted was that of 'orderly marketing'. This meant in practice seeking to open up gradually the markets of the wealthier fully-industrialised countries (FICs) to the imports, (particularly of manufactured goods), from the developing countries without disrupting unduly the economies and industrial structures of the importing countries. It was hoped, rather optimistically, to accommodate these conflicting concepts from world economic growth.

The basic objectives of the GATT are:

1. to eliminate quota restrictions;
2. to reduce tariffs progressively;
3. to remove restrictive non-tariff barriers to trade;
4. to ensure that measures applied to one are applied equally to all;
5. to ensure that any remaining protective measures are transparent to all.

The cornerstone of the GATT is known as the 'most favoured nation' principle (MFN). This lays down that whatever advantage, favour, privilege or immunity is granted or restriction applied by one member to another member shall be granted or applied immediately and unconditionally to all other members. Whatever else might have changed over the years in the practices of the GATT (and not all the changes have been for the better), the MFN principle has been the binding one which has held it together.

Under the GATT, much has been achieved since 1948. In particular, tariffs have been reduced progressively under a number of negotiating 'rounds' each of which takes several years to finalise: the Dillon Round in the 1950s; the Kennedy Round in the 1960s; the Tokyo Round in the 1970s. Currently negotiations towards a further round – called the Uruguay Round – are in progress.

In addition, the GATT permits many of the richer fully industrialised countries to operate their own unilateral 'general scheme of preferences' (GSP). Under these schemes, the importing countries take in from the less-developed countries certain quantities of goods in a wide range of food, raw material and manufactured categories either free of duty or at lower tariff rates. Admittedly, in some categories, the tariff-free quotas are not particularly generous but, to small and medium-sized countries with embryonic industries, these concessions can be very valuable. They also offer advantages to individual importing companies who are fast on their feet at the New Year.

Progress has also been made in reducing non-tariff barriers to trade such as subsidy support, countervailing duties (ostensibly to penalise dumping), complex import licensing procedures, technical regulations concerning product standards and customs valuation practices. However, in the main, GATT activity has been confined to manufactured goods. Little or no progress has been made in bringing agriculture (which accounts for 11 per cent of world trade), service invisibles (which account for 24 per cent) or government procurement under its rules.

Although much progress has been made, even more still remains to be done. Apart from extending the scope of the Agreement to cover agriculture and services there are still a number of outstanding problems to be resolved, for example:

1. Certain GATT members, such as Hong Kong and Taiwan, although still poor in terms of wealth per capita, have developed selectively some highly sophisticated industries which are able to compete disruptively with the industries of their customer countries. There is a move afoot to recategorise them formally as newly-industrialised countries (NICs) and require them to play their part in helping to solve the problems of the lesser-developed countries.
2. There are both security and moral problems in the trade in armaments;

a trade, however, which is critical to the commercial viability of certain 'sunrise' industries.
3. There is the question of the terms on which GATT members should trade with the Soviet Bloc.

In the current Uruguay Round, besides further tariff reductions, members are seeking to bring agriculture and services within the GATT ambit.

In these complex negotiations there are no clearcut solutions, nor any one single right path to tread. International trade is a highly emotive subject, particularly at times of recession or other stress, such as the current disputes between the United States, Japan and the EEC over discrepancies in their balances of trade running into tens of billions of pounds. At such times, negotiations can all too easily become 'a dialogue of the deaf'. On current form, the best that can be expected, in the short term at least, is a series of grudging and unsatisfactory compromises to keep trade flowing. What is certain however, is that, after the oil crisis of 1973, without the GATT there could all too easily have been a wholesale, worldwide regression into the protectionist practices of the 1930s.

Further details of the operation of the GATT, with special emphasis on its impact on importers, are given in section 4.2.

1.2.5 The European Economic Community

The event which finally completed Britain's transition from a nineteenth-century colonial power into a twentieth-century industrialised trading nation was her accession to the European Economic Community in 1973.

Originally, the EEC had been brought into being under the Treaty of Rome in 1959 by six of the richest nations in Europe – West Germany, France, Italy, Holland, Belgium and Luxembourg – the last three smaller nations having already formed a loose economic relationship under the name of Benelux. At this stage, Britain elected not to join. The EEC followed the success of the European Iron and Steel Community which was set up in 1951 by the same group of countries to create a common market in those two products. The EEC was at heart a customs union, designed to promote internal self-sufficiency and intra-trade. 'Intra-trade' is the jargon word for trade within the Community as opposed to 'external trade' which is trade across the Community borders with non-members. What basically happened was that the Community retreated behind a common customs tariff (CTT), which was levied on goods from non-members crossing its ultimate borders. The intention was that, once goods had crossed the common frontier, they would circulate freely within the Community. It still does not work quite like that!

The Treaty of Rome also established five main institutions for regulating and progressing the aims of the Community:

1. the Commission, (which is roughly comparable to a civil service);
2. the Council of Ministers, (roughly equivalent to the Cabinet);
3. the European Assembly (roughly comparable with the House of Commons but without its sovereign, law-making powers);
4. the Economic and Social Committee, (a kind of non-elected senate comprising experts and specialists from the member states);
5. the European Court of Justice, (not unlike the United States' Supreme Court in function).

The revenue of the Community is derived from the proceeds of the Common External Tariff (less the cost of national customs services which collect it) and 1.4 per cent of each member state's VAT collection. Fortunately, unlike national governments, the Community has no powers to borrow directly to cover overspending on its budget. This concentrates the mind of the Community's institutions on ensuring that each year's budget is balanced because, of course, the revenue side is fixed by the value of the prescribed sources.

The Community's founders knew their history and understood from the very beginning that a simple customs union was not enough. They had in their historical memory the ill-fated *Zollverein* established by the German states in the middle of the nineteenth century, which had demonstrated all too clearly how, if tariffs alone were removed, each member of the union vied with the other in the creation of imaginative non-tariff barriers to regulate trade in its favour. Therefore, from the beginning, the Treaty of Rome set out to secure that such barriers were also brought under control. To achieve this, the Commission was designated as the 'Custodian of the Treaty'. This meant that it had the sole right to propose and frame the specific measures which ensured that the aims of the Treaty were achieved.

The European Assembly and the Economic and Social Committee have the right to be consulted on the Commission's draft proposals but no right either to amend or to reject them outright. In practice, the drafts are sent to each institution for their opinions and are at once referred to one of their standing committees. These committees appoint one of their members as rapporteur to draft the opinion. It is that opinion and not the substance of the draft itself which is then debated and, after due amendment and ratification, sent to the Council of Ministers. The Council, which represents the national interests of the member states then either agrees to the proposal or returns it to the Commission with recommendations that it be redrafted. Then it goes round again, and round and round.

The Commission's proposals take two main forms:

1. *regulations*, which, once accepted by the Council of Ministers, become immediately part of the law of member states as they stand; and
2. *directives*, which are binding on each member state in their intent but leave each member state free, subject to the Commission's approval, to implement it in any way it chooses. It can either amend one of its existing laws, write a new law or, in certain cases, introduce a properly regulated code of practice.

The method which the Commission is required to use to eliminate non-tariff barriers is called 'harmonisation'. This concept is very important to the procedures of the Community (*see* section 4.3.2.). The framework of harmonisation comprises a number of 'common policies' which are assigned to the relevant divisions or 'directorates' of the Commission. The four main common policies relate to agriculture, finance, commerce and social issues. Thus the structure of the Community can most easily be visualised as a kind of Greek temple, the base of which is the customs union, the pillars the common policies and the roof the harmonisation measures.

The original intention was to develop each of these common policies in parallel. Unfortunately, in the early days, informed opinion was preaching that, at the current rate of population growth, there would be a massive and chronic world food shortage by the end of the century. Therefore the earliest concern of the Community was to make itself as self-sufficient in food as possible. This priority accorded particularly well with the interests of the powerful farm lobbies in West Germany, France and Italy. The result was the Common Agricultural Policy – the CAP (*see* section 4.3.4).

Today the Community resembles not so much an elegantly-proportioned Greek temple as a precariously tilted building in imminent danger of collapse. Fortunately, everybody in the Community, except possibly France, agrees that 'something must be done'. But precisely what? The ghosts of the founding fathers must be congratulating themselves on their original far-sightedness in denying the Community the ability to borrow its way out of such problems.

In 1959, there were four main reasons why Britain declined to join the EEC:

1. She still felt her main trading interest lay in continuing her trading links with the Commonwealth markets, particularly in their role as suppliers of cheap basic foodstuffs.
2. She placed a high value on what she saw as her 'special relationship' with the United States of America.
3. She was not particularly enthusiastic about the original Community concept of federation, with all the sacrifice of sovereignty and self-determination which the idea implied.

4. She was concerned in particular that Community rules would prevent her from propping up with subsidies and other protective devices her traditional, but increasingly uncompetitive and declining industries of textiles, steel, shipbuilding, automobiles and capital machinery.

As an alternative to EEC membership, Britain put together a much less restrictive confederation of the remaining European countries under the title of the European Free Trade Association (EFTA), The membership comprised Britain, Austria, Norway, Sweden, Denmark, Switzerland and Iceland. Although it was designated as a free trade area, it was *not* a customs union: that is to say, it did not have a common external tariff and each member held on to its tariff revenues. From the beginning, EFTA lacked both idealism and dynamism. Apart from Britain, the members, although rich, were small and reasonably self-contained.

In the course of time, the EEC gradually became more pragmatic and in the process lost many of its original ideals about becoming a fully-federated 'United States of Europe'. In the meantime, Britain found that, instead of being the most powerful trading nation in the world, she was now a medium-sized nation with an ageing industrial base. Furthermore, she found herself increasingly with no access of right to the three powerful consuming blocs each with internal free trading markets of over 250 million – the United States, The EEC and Comecon (the Soviet-led organisation of Eastern European state-trading nations). As such, her influence and negotiating ability in such organisations as the GATT, where international trade policy was being made and regulated, was waning rapidly. In particular, she was finding that, from outside the EEC, she had no way of ensuring that her interests were taken into account when new Community legislation, and especially harmonisation measures were being introduced. The dangers of being progressively excluded from the European market as a result of such measures became increasingly apparent.

In 1973, after long drawn out negotiations, Britain, along with Eire and Denmark, left EFTA and joined the Community. The long struggle as a new member to shape the Community to her own interests began, but, as the founder members were soon to discover, this time from inside and as of right. However, exposed to the tariff-free competition from the well-established and modern industrial base of the Community, the reality of Britain's industrial decline became manifest. Although, by 1986, half of her overseas trade was being done with the Community, she was running an annual trade deficit with the other member-states of more than £3 billion, and this would have been even greater but for the benefit of North Sea oil.

Since 1973, three other European countries – Greece, Spain and Portugal – have joined the Community and it is now the most powerful trading bloc in the world. Together its members account for over one-third of world trade, about half of which is intra-community.

The Commission, under the terms of the Treaty, carries out all trade negotiations with the outside world on behalf of its member states, acting under mandates which the members have ratified. The only exception to this is in the GATT assembly where, because the GATT was formed before the EEC, the EEC members retain their individual places and the Commission has an additional presence. The EEC Directorate responsible for external trade negotiations is Directorate-General I, but the detailed administration of the trade flow belongs to the Customs Union Service. Today, visible external trade accounts for some 25 per cent of the Community's total national product compared with 8 per cent in America and 12 per cent in Japan.

2

GOVERNMENT TRADE DEPARTMENTS

2.1 THE STRUCTURE OF GOVERNMENT

The policies of the government of the United Kingdom are implemented by its Civil Service, organised into a number of departments of state, each with a political head, who is usually a cabinet minister, and an administrative head, who is a civil servant, usually holding the rank of Permanent Secretary.

Today's top civil servants are the product of the Northcote-Trevelyn Report of 1853, which identified the need to recruit by public examination an administrative class of 'generalists of high calibre, educated at universities in studies which have no immediate connection with the business of any profession or government'. Over 100 years later, in 1986, a further report – by the Fulton Committee – made recommendations for dragging the higher echelons of the Civil Service into the twentieth century which the Service managed to bury without trace. In 1987, its style still bears an uncomfortable resemblance to the BBC's *Yes, Minister* series which seeks to parody it.

The great departments of state divide themselves into two mainly adversarial groups – the Treasury and the rest, popularly known as the 'spending departments'. The Treasury is responsible for implementing the fiscal and financial policies of the government of the day (whom it knows familiarly as GOD), for collecting the revenues needed to carry out those policies and for rationing those revenues between the spending departments. The spending departments, with the possible exception of the Foreign and Commonwealth Office, take their place in the pecking order of power and influence according to how much they are able to prise loose from a parsimonious Treasury. In this battle, each Permanent Secretary fights his departmental corner vigorously and without quarter. The great spending departments are Employment, Environment (which seeks somewhat desperately to control local authority spending), Education and Science, Health and Social Security, and Defence. Trade and Industry figures comparatively low in the pecking order of spenders.

For the purpose of collecting revenue, the Treasury uses two subsidiary services – Inland Revenue, which collects direct taxes such as income and corporation tax, and Customs and Excise, which collects indirect taxes, such as import duties and value added tax.

2.2 HM CUSTOMS AND EXCISE

2.2.1 History

Until 1909, the Customs and the Excise were two separate services. Customs was responsible for collecting duties and other dues on imported goods and Excise was responsible for collecting levies on certain nominated goods produced and processed in the United Kingdom such as wine, spirits, beer, tobacco and hydrocarbon products. In order to bring imports of excisable goods to competitive terms with the equivalent domestic products, a countervailing duty equivalent to the excise charge was imposed on them. Initially, excise officers were responsible for collecting these levies on entry, acting independently of customs officers.

Of the two taxes, customs is appreciably the older, the first legal record of its existence being contained in the 'New Custom of 1275'. It was a royal tax, imposed to raise revenue for wars and to contribute to the Privy Purse. For hundreds of years, the collection of it was 'farmed out' to private concessionaires and subject to much abuse in the form of fraud and smuggling. Eventually it was laid down that, as today, goods could only be imported legally through nominated points of entry, each being the responsibility of a Collector. It was not until 1671 that the farming of customs ceased, to be replaced by a government service very similar to today's. In contrast, the excise was a parliamentary tax, first levied during the Civil War to provide revenue for the Roundhead forces.

Throughout their separate histories, Customs and Excise officials were generally of high quality and status, numbering among their ranks Chaucer, Tom Paine, William Congreve, Robert Burns and Adam Smith (whose famous textbook on economics *The Wealth of Nations*, laid down that the first law of taxation was that it should not cost more to collect than it yields. In fact, Customs and Excise taxes are so efficient that, throughout their history, they have rarely cost more than 1 per cent of their revenues to administer.)

In the early 1920s, the collection of import duties was transferred from the Excise to the Customs Service, leaving Excise to concentrate on collecting dues on the nominated domestically-produced goods, the manufacturers of which were required to obtain a licence to operate.

The Customs Service has, from the earliest times included in its ranks an elitist, mostly uniformed anti-smuggling force known as the 'Waterguard', with its distinctive portcullis cap badge.

2.2.2 Structure and functions

When finally in 1908 the separate Royalist/Parliamentary rivalries were overcome, the two services merged into HM Customs and Excise, with an overall Board of Commissioners and 21 geographical administrative areas known as 'Collections', each under a Collector, with a total staff today of about 25,000.

In 1973, a new indirect tax, value added tax (VAT), replaced the much-criticised purchase tax as a method of taxing consumer expenditure (*see* section 7.1.2.). The responsibility for this was given to Customs and Excise. Today, Customs and Excise is responsible for:

1. collecting domestic excise duties and VAT on behalf of the UK government;
2. collecting external customs and excise duties and agricultural levies on behalf of the European Community;
3. enforcing prohibitions and restrictions on imports and exports;
4. protecting society from drugs, weapons and disease;
5. collecting trade statistics on behalf of the Department of Trade and Industry;
6. facilitating the freest possible movement of people and goods across UK frontiers.

2.3 THE DEPARTMENT OF TRADE AND INDUSTRY

2.3.1 History

From its inception, the Board of Trade has been a committee of the Privy Council – the body of the good and the great which advises the Sovereign. In 1672, the 'Committee of the Privy Council for Trade and Plantations' was established by patent and made responsible for examining commercial treaties, for regulating weights, measures and coinage and for encouraging the development of fisheries and overseas settlement. In 1710, it was also made responsible for collecting trade statistics from British consulates. Although it was disbanded in 1782, it was reformed as the Board of Trade in 1786 and given responsibility 'for co-ordinating all matters relating to trade'. To this end, it had oversight of commercial treaties, tariff negotiations with other countries and the British tariff system. It was in the front line of the great free trade debate in the mid-nineteenth century and, through this, became closely associated with the Customs Service.

As the nineteenth century progressed, the duties of the Board changed from trade policy adviser to a more executive role, particularly as it was given responsibility for regulating and registering newly-emerging commercial companies. It also acted as adviser to the Foreign Office in all matters concerning commerce and industry. In 1850, it was given responsibility for merchant shipping and, in 1920, for civil aviation. In 1886, it began to publish the *Board of Trade Journal* which was the forerunner of today's *British Business* magazine. After the First World War, it gradually assumed responsibility for consumer protection in all its manifestations. In 1918, a Departmental Committee was established within the Board of Trade to deal with trade monopolies and the development of new initiatives and research among British Industry.

During the Second World War, the Board took over responsibility for regional industrial policy and afterwards concentrated on expanding exports and controlling imports. It was the foremost department in negotiations leading to the signing of the GATT (*see* section 1.2.4) in 1947 and later played an important role in Britain's entry into the Common Market. Nowadays it has officials resident in many embassies and consulates throughout the world.

As a result of this expansion of responsibilities, the departments within the Board became increasingly autonomous and co-ordination between them correspondingly difficult. In 1970, there was a major reorganisation of government departments which sought to merge the proliferation of smaller independent ministries into a number of super-departments 'designed to resolve conflicts within line management rather than by inter-departmental compromise'. In this reorganisation, the Board of Trade was merged with part of the Ministry of Technology and became the Department of Trade and Industry (DTI). The historic title of President of the Board of Trade was retained by the new Secretary of State and, within the Department, the Board of Trade remained as a Privy Council committee.

In 1972, the function of collating and publishing trade statistics provided by Customs and Excise was computerised and transferred to the DTI's Business Statistics Office at Newport in Wales. In 1982, the DTI's responsibility for civil aviation and shipping was transferred to the Department of Transport and, in 1985, responsibility for small firms and tourism was transferred to the Department of Employment.

2.3.2 Structure and functions

The DTI, in its present form, is responsible for:

1. the implementation of trade policy at home and overseas;
2. the encouragement of investment, innovation and marketing skills and the promotion of international competitiveness in the UK industrial and commercial sectors;
3. the improvement of Britain's technological base;
4. the maintenance of the government's relationship with the United Kingdom's industrial and commercial sectors, both public and private; and
5. advising the Foreign and Commonwealth Office on commercial issues.

The political head of the department is the Secretary of State, who is a member of the Cabinet. He is assisted by three Under-secretaries of State and two Ministers. All but one of these are concerned with industry and consumer affairs.

The Minister for Trade is responsible for overseas trade policy and for liaison with the European Community on trade and commercial matters. He is also in charge of the Exports Guarantee Scheme and the British Overseas Trade Board, which provide support for British exporters, although export promotion itself is in the hands of one of the Under-secretaries.

Administratively, the Department is divided into 29 line and ten service divisions. Of these. *Division 24* is responsible for European commercial and industrial policy, including the harmonisation project for completing the internal market (*see* section 4.3.2). *Division 25* is responsible for international trade policy, (including the GATT, the Multi Fibre Arrangement and the General Scheme of Preferences), for import licensing, for protective action against disruptive imports, for anti-dumping investigations and for rules of origin. Both divisions of the **Department of Trade and Industry** are located at 1 Victoria Street, London SW1H 0ET (telephone 01-215 7877). *Division 26* is responsible for consumer affairs and is located at Millbank Tower, Millbank, London SW1P 4QU (telephone 01-211 7000). The DTI also maintains regional offices at Newcastle, Leeds, Manchester, Birmingham, Nottingham, Bristol, Glasgow, Cardiff and Belfast and district offices at Liverpool, Cleveland, Plymouth and Colwyn Bay.

3

THE STRUCTURE OF INTERNATIONAL TRADE

3.1 THE CLASSIFICATION OF TRADING NATIONS

Broadly speaking, there are two basic trading systems in the world – the state trading system and the open market system. Within each system, trade flows relatively freely to the agreed rules, but between the two systems trade tends to be uneasy and erratic.

3.1.1 The state trading system

Under the state trading system, which is used predominantly by the socialist states of Eastern Europe, trade flows are determined by the needs, interests and state planning procedures of the governments concerned. External trade with the rest of the world depends mainly on the requirement of those governments to control foreign currency flows.

For the most part, the state trading nations (STNs) conduct their external trade through a number of government-controlled trading agencies, each specialising in a particular product category. These agencies determine what is bought and sold, at what prices and on what terms and act as a buffer between the manufacturers and the foreign purchasers: direct dialogue between the two principal parties is rarely permitted or encouraged. They are, to all intents and purposes, extensions of their country's consular services whose policies are laid down rigidly in the periodic state economic plans. Therefore, in seeking to trade with STNs, it is useful to obtain some insight into the priorities contained in these Plans and this information can be best obtained from the British embassy in the country concerned.

The leading STNs are Bulgaria, Czechoslovakia, German Democratic Republic, Hungary, Poland, Romania and the Soviet Union. These countries, with the exception of Romania, are grouped together into the equivalent of a free trade area along the lines of EFTA which is called the Council for Mutual Economic Assistance (Comecon). Comecon was set up in 1949, with Cuba, Mongolia, and later, Vietnam as associate members.

The most important business of Comecon is the exchange of Russian oil and natural gas for Eastern European manufactured goods. However, it is more profitable for the non-Soviet members to sell to Western Europe and this they are permitted to do, under strict state control. Comecon does not recognise the existence of the EEC and insists on negotiating separately with each member state. There is also, for historical reasons, a special relationship between the two German republics which lead to extensive trading between them, usually in the form of outward processing (*see* section 3.4.2).

Other STNs which are not members of Comecon are China, Yugoslavia, Vietnam, North Korea and Albania. Certain of the emerging African countries which have socialist regimes also trade in a similar fashion to the more established STNs.

Trading with STNs can often be fraught with difficulties as both supplies and prices can be erratic and awareness of the needs of Western markets is often weak. Frequently, they seek to establish barter arrangements in preference to cash deals (*see* section 3.4.3) and to establish joint ventures involving technology transfers. There are also extremely sensitive strategic complications when high technology is involved. Import procedures for STNs are discussed in more detail in section 6.4.2.

3.1.2 The open market system

The rest of the world operates, in the main, under the principles of the market economy. Trading is conducted directly between suppliers and their overseas customer, or through their own specialist agents, with trade flows being dictated principally, but certainly not exclusively, by commercial supply and demand.

For all practical purposes, the open market system comprises the 92 nations which have signed the General Agreement on Tariffs and Trade (*see* section 1.2.4). However these nations cover a wide spectrum of economic development and so, not surprisingly, there is a wide divergence of opinion about what precisely constitutes fair, free and orderly trading. Therefore the GATT membership breaks down, for the purpose of negotiating changes, into a number of sub-groups each with common interests as follows:

1. *Fully-industrialised countries (FICs)* which are the rich nations of the Northern Hemisphere and Australasia with high GNPs and sophisticated industrial, commercial and financial systems, many of them former colonial powers.
2. *Newly-industrialised countries (NICs)*, which, although still poor in an overall sense by any measure, have developed industries which, in their

sophistication and marketing skills bear comparison with those of the FICs.
3. *Less-developed countries (LDCs)*, which are still predominantly poor and backward but have established one or two dominant industries which are so competitive as to threaten to disrupt specific sensitive sectors of the domestic markets of most FICs. These are again sub-divided into oil-producing and non-oil-producing countries.
4. *Lesser-developed countries (LDDCs)*, which are still in the earliest stages of industrialisation or have no manufacturing capacity at all, and as such do not constitute a threat to the industrial structures of the FICs but who need badly the revenue from selling their indigenous raw materials on the world markets.

The main division of interest lies between the rich FICs and the other groups of poorer developing countries, located mainly in Africa, the Carribean, South America and the Pacific. This clash of interests is known as the North–South dialogue. The situation is further aggravated by the fact that the three groups of developing countries, being at different stages of their development, frequently find themselves at odds with each other when it comes to negotiating changes in the present pattern of world trade with the FICs.

The traditional trading pattern between these FICs and the LDCs used to be cheap foodstuffs and raw materials from the LDCs exchanged for manufactured capital and consumer goods from the FICs, with the distribution of the added values which resulted very much in favour of the FICs. Today however, almost all the LDCs are seeking to advance their development by creating industrial infrastructures using the capital goods exported by the FICs to exploit their indigenous raw materials and cheap labour. In GATT negotiations therefore, they are attempting both to protect their own domestic markets as outlets for their emerging industries and to open up the markets of the FICs in order to obtain further foreign currency with which to continue their expansion. On the other side, the FICs wish to continue to sell sophisticated manufactured products to what they regard as their traditional markets but are extremely reluctant to open their own markets more widely to the highly competitive consumer goods which these exports help to produce.

Aside from these countries, both developed and developing, which fall fairly obviously into one or the other of these categories, there are a small number of countries with an ambivalent status and trading identity, the most prominent of which are Israel, South Africa, and Taiwan. These have an economic profile somewhere between that of and FIC of NIC, with above-average wealth and a sophisticated manufacturing base but, for political reasons, they are not accepted as negotiating members by the main interest groupings. A list of the open market trading countries, together with their various trading affiliations is shown in Appendix F.

When the GATT negotiating 'rounds' are in progress, these broad sub-groupings form themselves into formidable lobbies, working to commonly-agreed 'negotiating mandates' and bargain hard. However, establishing such group mandates presents the individual countries with 'an option of difficulties'. Under pressure, emotive arguments about sovereignty arise all too easily, and more especially in multi-party democracies where opposition parties are disinclined to allow the governing party to bind them to policies and arrangements which they may wish to repudiate on coming to power. The process of achieving a group negotiating mandate is tedious and long-winded and, even when it is achieved, is inclined to make the negotiators appear flat-footed and inflexible when the inevitable process of 'trading off' begins.

3.1.3 Formal open market groupings

Apart from these alignments which accord with commercial and economic interest, two sub-groups within the GATT have formal constitutions – the European Community and the European Free Trade Area (*see* section 1.2.5).

There have been other attempts among the developing countries to create similar customs unions and free trade areas, notably in the Pacific Basin, the Carribean and South America. The difficulties of doing so are perhaps best illustrated by the grouping known as the Association of East Asian Nations (ASEAN) which was first established in 1977. Currently ASEAN comprises Singapore, Malaysia, Indonesia, Thailand, the Philippines and Brunei. Its long-term objective is to create a full customs union along the lines of the European Community, but, so far, progress has been painfully slow. Only some 17 per cent of the Association's total trade takes the form of intra-association trade (compared with 53 per cent of intra-trading within the EEC). Their exports are heavily biased towards oil, liquid gas and raw materials and 45 per cent of their external trade is done with Japan and the United States of America (two nations renowned for the rapidity of their protective reactions if things start to get out of hand). Furthermore, Singapore is already a tariff-free area whereas the other members have high and widely-disparate tariff structures, so the possibility of a common external tariff seems a long way off.

In South and Central America, there are currently three such organisations:

1. *The Latin American Free Trade Association (LAFTA)*, whose members are Argentina, Colombia, Bolivia, Brazil, Chile, Ecuador, Mexico, Paraguay, Uruguay and Venezuela.
2. *The Central American Common Market (ODECA)*, whose members are El Salvador, Guatemala, Honduras, Nicaragua and Costa Rica.
3. *The Caribbean Common Market (Caricom)*, whose members are Antigua, Bahamas, Barbados, Belize, Dominica, Grenada, Guyana, Jamaica, Montserrat, St Kitts-Nevis, St Lucia, St Vincent and the Grenadines and Trinidad and Tobago.

In the Arabian Gulf, there is also an embryonic Free Trade Area comprising Saudi Arabia, Kuwait, Qatar, Oman and the United Arab Emirates. They are all members of OPEC and, in terms of tariffs at least, are already free traders. Currently, they are seeking reciprocal arrangements with their external trading partners in products such as petrochemicals, but have not yet shown any inclination to convert their Free Trade Area into a Common Market along the lines of the European Community.

All are experiencing difficulties comparable with those of the ASEAN group and indeed the European Community, notably in the field of harmonisation of commercial and economic practices which impinge on the free circulation of trade within the group.

Nevertheless, the trend is there. If common markets can be achieved among groupings of the weaker nations and intra-community trade within each group encouraged from behind common tariff barriers, then the advantages to them in terms of increased international negotiating strength is manifest.

It seems reasonable to assume that, some time during the next century, the world could find itself divided into a number of such groupings, each with a strong intra-community trade, a relative degree of self-sufficiency and common tariff barriers, capable of standing up to the superpowers in organisations such as the GATT. This is probably the best hope we have for freer international trade based on orderly marketing principles in the long run.

3.1.4 The Organisation for Economic Co-operation and Development (OECD)

The other formal grouping which occurs among the richer and more sophisticated fully industrialised countries is the OECD which has the following membership:

Australia	Greece	Norway
Austria	Iceland	Portugal

Belgium	Eire	Spain
Canada	Italy	Sweden
Denmark	Japan	Switzerland
Finland	Luxembourg	Turkey
France	The Netherlands	United Kingdom
W. Germany	New Zealand	United States

The EEC member states are members of OECD in their own right because OECD was formed before the Community. The EEC Commission has an additional seat on the Organisation's Council. Yugoslavia is in partial membership.

The stated aims of the OECD are as follows:

1. to achieve economic growth and rising living standards among member states;
2. to maintain financial stability;
3. to contribute to the sound economic expansion of the Third World;
4. to further the expansion of trade on a multi-national, non-discriminatory basis.

The OECD has the following structure:

1. a Council, which acts as a focus for general discussion but rarely takes policy decisions involving members in specific undertakings to act;
2. a number of special committees, which keep the policies of member states under review and prepare guidelines for appropriate measures of co-ordination.
3. a Secretariat, of some 1,300 based in Paris.

Within OECD's broader membership, there is an exclusive 'club' known as the 'Group of Five' (G 5) – the United States of America, Japan, West Germany, Britain and France. The Group seeks, with little reference to other OECD members, to achieve agreement between themselves on the regulation of their balance of payments through the manipulation of exchange and interest rates and other fiscal regulatory mechanisms. At times it is expanded into the 'Group of Seven' by the inclusion of Canada and Italy.

Although OECD's influence on specific trade issues and negotiations is largely indirect, it is none the less a powerful and persuasive caucus for forwarding the interests of the richer nations. In particular, its periodic economic forecasts for the world economy can be very influential in macro-economic decision making.

3.1.5 The ex-colonial networks

There are other types of national groupings which do not attempt to create customs unions or free trade areas. These, in the main, take the form of special relationship networks between the fully industrialised countries and their former colonial dependencies. The most prominent of these is the Lomé Convention grouping (*see* section 3.2.2).

3.1.6 Generalised schemes of preference

The main exceptions to these ex-colonial clubs are the generalised schemes of preference (GSPs) which are operated by many of the leading industrialised nations. The GSP system was developed in 1968 under the auspices of the United Nations Conference on Trade and Development (UNCETAD). These schemes are designed to increase the exporting opportunities for some 150 developing countries by offering them a range of preferential tariff advantages. They have been authorised by the GATT as special and acceptable derogations to its general principle of equal treatment for all (known more generally as 'most favoured nation' treatment (MFN).

GSPs have the following characteristics:
1. They are non-discriminatory, that is to say their benefits are accorded to all developing countries without distinction.
2. They are unilateral, that is to say they are offered to beneficiary countries by the developed countries without any negotiation being involved.
3. They are non-reciprocal, that is to say the beneficiary countries are not required to grant corresponding or offset benefits in return.

Although, as a result of cumulative tariff cuts made in successive GATT rounds, tariffs are becoming less and less significant in encouraging and regulating international trade, GSPs do provide a useful advantage to developing countries.

From an importer's point of view, the GSP offers inducements to purchase competitively from the LDCs. However, preferential tariffs on the more frequently traded industrial products are subject to ceiling limitations. Once these are reached, all subsequent shipments are liable to the full rate of duty. There is a separate arrangement for agricultural products. The GSP operated by the European Community is described in detail in section 3.2.3.

3.2 THE EEC SPECIAL RELATIONSHIP NETWORK

3.2.1 Association agreements

Under Article 113 of the Treaty of Rome, the EEC Commission has the responsibility of negotiating trade agreements on behalf of all member states, working to negotiating mandates ratified by the Council of Ministers. Since 1969, as a result of these negotiations, the Community has entered into a series of association agreements with EFTA and a network of other countries, many of them former colonies of member states.

The Special Relations Agreement with EFTA allows for free trade in industrial goods (with special terms for a small number of sensitive products) but not for agricultural products. After the accession to the EEC of the United Kingdom, Denmark, Eire and Portugal, the countries remaining in membership of EFTA are Austria, Norway, Finland, Sweden and Switzerland.

Other association agreements have been signed with:

Algeria	Egypt	Malta	Tunisia
Cyprus	Israel	Morocco	Turkey

who are known collectively as the 'Mediterranean Associates'. and with:

Argentina	India	Mexico	Syria
Bangladesh	Jordan	Pakistan	Uruguay
Brazil	Lebanon	Sri Lanka	Yugoslavia

all of which offer some form of preference and trade co-operation, together, in some cases with aid. The agreements are in a number of versions, but, in the main, offer trade on varying preferential terms. The agreement with Turkey, in particular, accepts it as a potential future member of the Community.

Importers who are considering doing business with these countries should make contact with the appropriate division of the Department of Trade and Industry.

3.2.2 The Lomé Convention

The most wide-ranging of the EEC's agreements is the Lomé Convention concluded with the 58 former colonies of member states and the 26 residual dependencies of Britain, France and the Netherlands in Africa, the Pacific and the Caribbean – a group known collectively as the ACP states.

The Convention allows for the following:

1. Duty-free access to the EEC for all industrial goods and all agricultural products not covered by the Common Agricultural Policy.

2. The establishment of two funds – one called STABEX which is designed to stabilise the prices of basic agricultural products, the other called SYSMON to do the same for minerals both of which commodities form the core of ACP exports to the Community.
3. ACP access to grants and loans from the European Development Fund on favourable terms.
4. A special deal for sugar imports from the Caribbean ACPs.

The Convention was renewed, with minor alterations, in 1985 for five years.

3.2.3. The EEC's generalised scheme of preferences

Finally, the EEC has its own generalised scheme of preferences which provides tariff benefits for 156 LDCs. This was renewed in 1986 for five years. The scheme provides for what are essentially two different regimes, one for industrial, the other for agricultural products.

In the industrial sector the scheme provides for the following:

1. Some 47 products are designated as 'sensitive' and, on these, quantitative limits are set on what can be imported free of duty. Once the ceiling limits are reached, full duty becomes payable on all subsequent imports.
2. On these products, the newly-industrialised countries (NICs) are granted individual duty-free quotas which are then rationed out amongst the member states according to a 'burden-sharing' formula. The United Kingdom's share is 14.5 per cent of total Community quota plus access to the Community reserve of 20 per cent. Once the quota has been used up, full duty must be re-imposed automatically.
3. Each LDC is subject to an individual duty-free ceiling for these products but these are not 'burden-shared' among the EEC member states. Once any ceiling is reached, member states may apply to have full duties re-imposed throughout the Community.
4. The remaining non-sensitive products – approximately 1,700 – are subject to import surveillance at the point of entry into the Community. If a member state considers imports in any category are growing at such a rate as to threaten disruption of its domestic market, then it can apply to the Community for the product to be reclassified as 'sensitive'; if the application is accepted the Commission will set a new duty-free ceiling.
5. There are special and more stringent arrangements for textile and clothing products and, in these cases, duty-free ceilings are linked to quotas established under the Multi-Fibre Arrangement (*see* section 4.2.5).

34   THE STRUCTURE OF INTERNATIONAL TRADE

In the agricultural sector the Scheme provides for the following:

1. Approximately 307 products, none of which is included in the Common Agricultural Policy regime, are subject either to reduced tariff rates or to total exemption.
2. There are no ceiling restrictions on these products (except in the case of tobacco, soluble coffee, cocoa butter and preserved pineapples).

The 38 lesser-developed countries (LDDCs) are granted exemption from duty for all products, both industrial and agricultural. Certain special conditions apply to Yugoslavia, China and Rumania. Currently, GSP beneficiaries account for some 40 per cent of total Community imports. Of these, only 11 per cent qualify for GSP treatment, and in fact, only 65 per cent of the preferences that can be claimed are utilised.

A condition for the granting of GSP rights is that the beneficiary country shall notify the Commission of the authority it has nominated to issue certificates of origin. Goods from countries which have not provided this notification cannot be accepted for GSP treatment. The scheme is reviewed annually by the Council of Ministers and details of any revisions are published in the *Official Journal of the EEC* and in *British Business – Notices to Importers* each January. The DTI has produced a booklet entitled *The General Scheme for Preferences – A Summary of the European Community Scheme 1987* which can be obtained from: **Industrial Trade Policy Division**, Room 457, The Department of Trade, 1 Victoria Street, London SW1H 0ET (telephone: 01-215 5467). Further information about the scheme itself, the status of beneficiary countries and quota availability can be obtained from: **I.C. Division C, Branch 5**, Adelaide House, London Bridge, London EC1R 9DB (telephone: 01-626 1515, ext. 2173 or 2453). Many of the LDCs are beneficiaries under both the Lomé and the GSP systems, a list of the beneficiaries of both are shown at Appendix F.

3.3 PATTERNS OF INTERNATIONAL TRADE

3.3.1 Trade flows in the international market

The most authoritative and comprehensive source of information concerning international trade in 'visibles' is the OECD monthly bulletin, *Statistics of Foreign Trade*. In particular, Part 3 deals with trade by commodity group and Part 4 deals with trade by source and destination.

Trade can be measured in terms of both imports and exports. In theory, the two sums should balance out because, after all, everybody's exports must end up somewhere. In practice, there is a discrepancy for three reasons:

1. Exports are evaluated at the price at which they are loaded on the ship

(FOB), whereas imports are evaluated with the cost of freight and insurance added (CIF).
2. There are substantial time-lags created whilst goods are in transit.
3. Not all countries declare all their trade in their statistical returns.

The overall difference in any one year is in the region of 8 per cent, the majority of which is probably attributable to freight and insurance charges. In analysing trade flows, it is usual to use the export stream only. The classification of trade flows by 'type of country' gives the broadest indication of how the flows are distributed. (This is shown in Table 3.1).

Table 3.1 Distribution of total world trade (per cent)

	within Group	with other Groups	Total
Developed countries	42	19	61
Comecon	5	5	10
LDCs – oil producers	1	13	14
– newly-industrialised	1	7	8
– others	3	4	7
Total	52	48	100
Of the developed countries 61 per cent share:			
EEC	33		
USA	12		
Japan	6		
Rest	10		
In terms of commodities the world total is:			
Agricultural products	13		
Fuel and raw materials	27		
Manufactured goods	60		

3.3.2 The structure of UK trade

Unfortunately, the United Kingdom uses two methods of calculating its international trading activity – one for balance of payments purposes and the other for overseas trade statistics. They are compared in Table 3.2. The significant difference between the two methods is that, in the balance of payments account, freight and insurance are counted as invisible trade and exports are adjusted accordingly. The balance of payments account includes invisible trade but the DTI's overseas trade statistics do not.

For a first perspective therefore, the relationship between visible and invisible trade balances revealed in the balance of payments current account is shown in Table 3.3. The analysis of trade flows in terms of destination and commodity is more readily available in the DTI's *Overseas Trade Statistics* but, in making comparisons between imports and exports, it must be

Table 3.2 Comparison of UK methods of calculating its international trade

	£ billion – 1985		
	Balance of payments current account	Overseas trade statistics	Difference
Exports	72.8	73.0	+0.2
Imports	81.3	86.1	+4.8
Difference	– 8.5	–13.1	

Table 3.3 The relationship between visibles and invisibles in the UK balance of payments current account

	£ billion – 1986		
	Visible trade	Invisible trade	Difference
Exports	72.8	n/a	
Imports	81.3	n/a	
Difference	– 8.5	+7.5	–1.0

remembered that imports in the OTS figures include carriage and freight. A digest of more detailed OTS figures is published quarterly in the DTI's magazine *British Business*.

The pattern of UK visible trade in 1986 by source and destination is shown in Table 3.4. This demonstrates:
1. a visible trade deficit of £13.0 billion;
2. the overwhelming advantage which membership of the large tariff-free community which the EEC offers to an industrialised country;
3. the need for continued access to the markets of rich, high-living countries which have the potential to absorb the output of Britain's manufacturing sector.

The pattern of UK trade by product category is shown in Table 3.5. This demonstrates:

1. the offset role which North Sea Oil is playing in narrowing the overall visible trade deficit;
2. how far Britain really is from being an 'oil economy' in the meaning of the term when applied to the OPEC countries;
3. the continuing importance of Britain's diminishing industrial export base;
4. the relative insignificance of the deficit in the agricultural and processed food, drink and tobacco sectors (indeed, if tobacco were to be excluded, the deficit would be roughly halved);
5. the relative insignificance of the impact of the EEC's inefficient and wasteful Common Agricultural Policy on the overall trade balance.

Table 3.4 UK visible trade by source and destination in 1986

	Exports £ billion	Imports £ billion	Difference	Exports %	Imports %
EEC	35.0	44.5	− 9.5	48.0	51.7
Rest of Europe	7.0	11.9	− 4.9	9.6	13.8
USA	10.4	8.5	+ 1.9	14.2	10.0
Other developed nations	5.8	8.6	− 2.8	8.0	10.0
Total developed nations	58.2	73.5	−15.3	79.8	85.5
State traders	1.7	2.0	− 0.3	2.3	2.3
Oil-producing LDCs	5.5	1.9	+ 3.6	7.5	2.2
Other LDCs	7.6	8.6	− 1.0	10.4	10.0
Total LDCs	13.1	10.5	+ 2.6	17.9	12.2
Grand total	73.0	86.0	−13.0	100.0	100.0

Table 3.5 UK visible trade by commodity in 1986

	Exports £ billion	Imports £ billion	Difference	Exports %	Imports %
Agriculture & fish	1.9	4.0	− 2.1	2.6	4.7
Energy					
Oil	8.2	4.2	+ 4.0	11.2	4.9
Non-oil	1.0	2.5	− 1.5	1.4	2.9
Total energy	9.2	6.7	+ 2.5	12.6	7.8
Materials & semi-Mfgrs					
Metals & minerals	6.7	7.9	− 1.2	9.2	9.1
Chemicals & fibres	10.0	7.7	+ 2.3	13.7	9.0
Total materials & semi-Mfgrs	16.7	15.6	+ 1.1	22.9	18.1
Finished goods					
Manufactured	38.5	50.0	−11.5	52.7	58.1
Food, drink & tobacco	4.2	7.7	− 3.5	5.8	9.0
Total finished goods	42.7	57.7	−15.0	58.5	67.1
Other goods & services	2.5	2.0	+ 0.5	3.4	2.3
Grand total	73.0	86.0	−13.0	100.0	100.0

More detailed information by country, both monthly and annual, is published in the booklet *Overseas Trade Statistics for the United Kingdom*, and by commodity, quarterly, in *Business Monitor MQ 10 – Overseas Trade Analysed in Terms of Industries*. Both publications can be obtained from HM Stationery Offices.

More detailed analysis of a particular sector, based on the bill of entry records, can be obtained on request for the price of the search fee from: **Bill of Entry Service, Statistical Office, HM Customs and Excise,** Portcullis

House, 27 Victoria Avenue, Southend-on-Sea SS2 6AL (telephone: Southend 49421, ext. 310).

Overall, the UK trade statistics hardly present the picture which might be anticipated of the world's first industrialised country with a high population density and a temperate climate. Britain appears to be more self-sufficient in foodstuffs and industrial materials and much less self-sufficient in finished consumer goods than might be expected from its historical and demographic profile. This 'snapshot' of the 1986 situation is confirmed also by the growth trends over the past 40 years or so, although macro-statistical patterns are very slow to respond to what might appear to be fast-changing economic situations. Furthermore, there is some evidence in the high ratio of invisible trade to finished manufactured goods that Britain is leading the way into the much heralded 'post-industrial society'.

On the other hand, again in perspective, this picture of a declining manufacturing base does not necessarily indicate a decline in that sector's efficiency. Being first to industrialise gave Britain an opportunity to dominate world trade and, for over half a century, the opportunity was seized with enthusiasm. Inevitably, however, as other nations developed their own industrial bases, they were bound to erode this dominance both by commercial competitiveness and by trade regulation. It has not been so much that Britain has become less efficient as that other nations have caught up with, and in some cases passed her. It is a sad fact of life that normally the 'me-too' operator, coming late into the market and thus being able to learn from the innovator's experience, does much better in the long haul.

So where does Britain go from here? Sadly also, the crystal ball has been replaced by the economic model: it is now a participant sport and anybody can join who can afford the price of a number-crunching computer.

3.4 SPECIAL FORMS OF TRADE

3.4.1 Entrepot trading

Entrepot trading is the term used to describe the situation when goods are sent to a country with the intention of re-exporting them without any change in their nature or addition to their intrinsic value. These goods are not classified as 'imported' because they are not subjected to the clearance procedures applied to goods which are destined for use or consumption in the country of passage. Entrepot trading arises because the 'country of passage' offers some special advantage in terms of storage, handling or marketing of bulk goods. Entrepot centres are in fact concentration and clearing points for smaller countries or specialist manufacturers who find it cheaper to use such facilities than to handle a widespread trading operation themselves.

Entrepot goods in transit from one country to another via an entrepot centre, may be held duty free in that centre under surveillance of Customs in a bonded warehouse. A warehouse is so described because the warehouse owner or an approved agent is required to put up a bond which guarantees payment of duty if the goods are deflected from re-export to the home market.

The leading entrepot centres are Rotterdam, Singapore and Hong Kong. The last two have, in fact, a trading through-put which is larger than their total Gross National Product. New competitors in the field for entrepot business are the freeports (*see* section 3.5.3).

Successful entrepot trading requires both substantial resources and an experience of markets on a worldwide scale. It is therefore conducted in the main by large, long-established general merchant houses such as the Far Eastern 'hongs'. Entrepot trade differs from outward and inward processing in that, because the goods remain unchanged, they normally retain their tariff classification and therefore their primary country of origin.

3.4.2 Outward and inward processing relief

These are known respectively as 'OPR' and 'IPR'. In the case of the United Kingdom, both reliefs are granted under an EEC scheme. The terms describe the system under which materials or components are shipped from one country to another for processing or incorporation into a new manufactured product and afterwards this finished product is returned to the exporting country. Because the EEC is a duty-free area, the relief only applies to transactions between member and non-member states when the question of duty does arise. 'Relief' covers both normal tariff duties and agricultural levies. In such circumstances, both the component exporter and the manufacturer in the processing country who intends to re-export the finished product can apply for exemption from duty and/or agricultural levies on that part of the value represented by the material or component incorporated into that product.

OPR/IPR is a particularly useful procedure to adopt with goods returned to the manufacturer for repair or alteration. OPR cannot be used if the faulty goods are replaced by new goods (*see* Customs Notice 235). Reliefs granted under these processes do not affect liability to pay VAT, which, if the re-importer is a registered taxable person, is payable at the relevant rate on the full value of the re-imported goods.

Outward processing relief (OPR) covers the situation when the trader who originally exports the materials or components claims relief from duty or agricultural levies on the value of those materials or components when he re-imports the finished goods. This means that he only pays duty on the value added during the manufacturing process. In the United Kingdom, relief procedures are laid down under the Import Duty (Outward Processing Relief) Regulations of 1976 and the Agricultural Levies (Outward Processing Relief) Order, also of 1976. The conditions for obtaining such relief are as follows:

1. Customs and Excise must give prior authorisation for the procedure to the trader before the materials or components are first exported.
2. The value of the exported goods must be clearly established.
3. On re-entry, Customs and Excise must be able to satisfy themselves that the declared quantities of the right materials are included in the finished product. This is normally established by defining the 'rate of yield' on the original application form. The 'rate of yield' is a calculation of the quantity of manufactured goods which can be made from a specific quantity of the material exported (e.g. how many handkerchiefs from a cotton fabric).

If the process of assembling or manufacturing the materials or components into finished products changes its tariff classification (as it normally would), then the country of origin changes to that of the manufacturer (*see* section 6.4.8).

Inward processing relief (IPR) is the reverse process to OPR, whereby a British manufacturer may claim relief from duties and levies on materials or components included in his finished product when he re-exports it or sells it to another IPR trader. There are two methods of claiming IPR:

1. Suspension, whereby the manufacturer does not have to pay duty on entry. This method is used when the manufacturer clearly intends to export his total production of the goods manufactured from the imported materials or components.
2. Drawback, whereby the manufacturer pays duty on the imports, but claims it back when the finished goods are re-exported. This method is used when the manufacturer is uncertain about how much of his production of the goods concerned will be re-exported and how much sold on the domestic market.

Under both schemes, the operation known as 'triangulation' is permitted. That is to say, the materials or components may be exported by one trader to the manufacturer and despatched by him to a different trader, either in the original member-state or in another. All such transactions qualify for relief.

Fuller details of import procedures and documentation are shown in section 6.4.6.

3.4.3 Countertrade

Countertrade is a term used for the sophisticated form of barter arrangement favoured by Eastern Bloc state trading nations in certain types of transactions. The two main problems with such arrangements are:

1. how to establish pricing parameters for each side of the agreement; and
2. how to dispose of any goods which are accepted from the STNs by traders who have little experience of trading in them in international markets.

To overcome this problem, a thriving exchange market for countertrade goods has grown up in Vienna. If an importer decides to enter into this form of trade, he will need to engage the services of one of the specialist 'brokers' who deal in this market. Advice can be obtained either from the international branch of his bank or, if he is in membership, from the British Importers' Confederation.

The four principal forms which countertrading takes are as follows:

1. *Barter arrangements*, where goods are exchanged directly for other goods without money being involved.
2. *Compensation agreements*, where a capitalist exporter sells goods or services required by an STN against a cash credit note which can be exchanged for consumer goods from different suppliers within the STN.
3. *Buyback agreements*, where a capitalist manufacturer supplies an STN firm with machinery and buys back a proportion of its output in exchange.
4. *Linkage agreements*, where each side accepts payment in the form of a parallel credit facility that can be traded in the course of negotiating future contracts with other parties. These balances are held in what are known as 'evidence accounts'.

All such agreements can be traded in Vienna with third parties on a discount basis either in the form of goods or credit-drawing facilities. Some of this trading takes the form of 'switch deals', under which Western traders buy the right to use non-convertible Eastern Bloc currency balances for 'hard' currencies and use them to purchase goods from the deficit state trading nations at a discount.

Transaction involving capital goods imported by STNs usually include technology transfer clauses, which, in the case of high-tech products, can be strategically sensitive, (particularly if US technology or patents are involved, even indirectly). In all cases the main problem arises in establishing pricing parameters for each side of the agreement, although discounting facilities available on the Vienna market provide a much-needed flexibility.

Currently, countertrading involves almost exclusively the Comecon members of the Eastern Bloc of STNs, but, with the new 'open door' policy of the Peoples' Republic of China, an increase in this type of trading with her can be expected. Although many traders do reasonably well by accepting such terms, the general experience is that if money had not already been invented it would be necessary to invent it, if only to oil the wheels of international trade.

3.5 CHANNELS OF TRADE

3.5.1 Direct importing – foreign manufacturer to distributor

In the chain of importation, a number of complex functions have to be performed with great precision and accuracy if the goods are to arrive without undue delay or incident (or, indeed, to arrive at all). These functions are as follows:

1. packaging goods on supplier's premises;
2. negotiating freighting method and timing;
3. preparing export and import documentation;
4. transporting goods to main terminal:
    a. docks for sea transport,
    b. airport for air transport,
    c. carrier or freight terminal for road/rail transport;
5. loading on to main method of transportation;
6. monitoring progress of transportation;
7. arranging customs passage if goods are to move through other countries;
8. unloading at port of entry;
9. customs clearance at point of entry (including payment of duties, levies and taxes);
10. payment for transportation and related services;
11. transportation from point of entry to importer's premises or other nominated address;
12. arrangement and payment of insurance against appropriate risks;
13. payment for goods.

Clearly it is essential, in establishing this chain, for the importer himself to make firm and specific contractual arrangements to cover all these functions and to establish with equal clarity the point at which the title of the goods passes from the supplier to himself. Generally speaking, and subject to satisfactory arrangements concerning payment for the goods, the title to the goods passes to the importer when the foreign supplier has discharged the appropriate set of responsibilities which he has contracted to perform.

To assist all parties involved in such transactions, the International Chamber of Commerce (ICC) has produced a *Guide to Incoterms No 354* which explains in detail the precise meaning and division of responsibilities between the supplier, the shipping agent and the importer. The Guide provides full explanations of the various 'shorthand' terms used in international trade to describe the division of responsibilities. This guide can be obtained from **International Chamber of Commerce**, Centre Point, 103 New Oxford Street, London WC1A 1QB. However, most chambers of commerce will hold a library copy of the Guide. A summary of the terms used to describe the shipment of goods by air, sea, rail and road transport is shown in Appendix A.

This range of possibilities provides the importer with a high degree of flexibility in determining the most competitive means of getting imported goods to his customers. The ICC also provides for its members a Court of Arbitration to adjudicate in disputes arising on these issues.

3.5.2 *The role of agencies and other import specialists*

Those who import on a small scale, for whom importing is a subsidiary activity and price is not the main factor, are well advised not to attempt to carry out the importing operation themselves.

The medium-sized importer who imports a relatively narrow range of goods from well-established sources could handle the administration of imports himself by building up an 'in-house' manual which lays down importing procedures for the specific goods in which he deals, having decided to take over responsibility at a particular point in the transportation chain (say C&F or ex ship). Providing that the importer is careful to take specialist advice in producing this manual then this latter option could well provide him with a cheap and flexible way of developing a competitive edge in his costing, even over the employment of a specialist agent and almost certainly over buying 'Delivered Duty Paid' or from a wholesale house.

Finally, the large-scale importer, who is buying a wide range of goods from a variety of sources either in order to wholesale or to support his retailing activities, almost certainly needs his own importing organisation.

If the decision is not to 'do it yourself', then basically there are two choices open as follows:

1. to buy shelf stock from import merchants or wholesalers; or
2. to buy from the local agents or subsidiary of overseas manufacturers.

Both methods are in effect, the same as buying from a domestic manufacturer.

The import merchant or wholesaler purchases goods from overseas sources on his own behalf, applies his mark-up and sells them delivered to distributors. He usually specialises in particular ranges of goods but can arrange to supply goods made to customers' specifications if necessary.

The import agent specialises in offering goods made by one or more overseas manufacturer and is paid on commission for doing so. They also participate in transporting and delivering the goods to their customers.

The local subsidiary normally sells internationally branded goods and, in addition to providing import administration and servicing, is responsible for local market promotion.

Any of these three sources is satisfactory and trouble free, but may not yield the most competitive prices. An intermediate solution is to employ the services of a Freight Forwarding Agent (FFA). An FFA is a kind of 'transportation broker'. He rarely owns his own transportation organisation directly, although he may be connected with such organisations, either as owner or owned. The services he can provide are as follows:

1. Advice on packing, routing, documentation and insurance from an up-to-date knowledge of rates, regulations, conditions and availability.
2. Quotations for these services from competing operators.
3. Performing the role of consolidation or groupage agent. That is to say, he can group together a number of smaller consignments from different clients into a larger consignment which will provide smaller-scale operators with the competitive advantage of bulk rates.
4. Clearance of goods through customs at both shipping points.
5. On this basis, provide a door-to-door service, over which he exercises control at all stages, or, alternatively, take responsibility for any part of the chain which the customer wishes to delegate to him.

There are several hundred freight forwarders and they have their own association which supervises operating standards, makes representations to governments and negotiates with other institutions on behalf of its members. Its address is **The Institute of Freight Forwarders**, Suffield House, 9 Paradise Road, Richmond, Surrey TW9 1SA (telephone: 01-948 3141). The Institute is able and willing to provide importers who might wish to use the services of its members with any help or information they need. The leading freight forwarders are also listed geographically in the British Importers Confederation's *Importers Handbook*, a copy of which can be obtained from **British Importers Confederation**, 69 Cannon Street, London EC4N 5AB, (telephone: 01-248 4444).

3.5.3. Free trade zones

In certain types of operation, notably those of an entrepot nature, considerable savings in both effort and cost can be achieved by using the facilities of a 'freeport' or, more accurately, 'free trade zone', because these zones can be located not only at seaports, but also at airports and, indeed, in any properly secured enclave.

By 1987, there were some 480 such zones located in 86 countries. The best known are the ports of Copenhagen, Rotterdam, Hamburg, Singapore and Hong Kong and the airports of Schipol (Amsterdam) and Shannon (Eire). In the United States of America alone there are 132 such zones and in Switzerland some 25. However, it must be said that the operating rules and advantages which this proliferation offers vary extensively.

In Britain, the first free trade zones were authorised, somewhat against the advice of the Treasury, in 1984 – three in seaport and three in airport locations. By January 1987, of the seaports, Liverpool had 37 traders using it and a 1986 throughput of £60m, Southampton had three users and a 1986 throughput of £15m, and, Cardiff has yet to start operations. Of the airports, Prestwick opened but has since closed down through lack of user support, Belfast is still awaiting Customs approval, and Birmingham finally opened in 1986 with one active and five potential users.

In a free trade zone, a specific area is set aside and secured, within which goods can be lodged. Goods may remain within the zones indefinitely without incurring duty, EEC levies or VAT providing that they are not consumed or do not change ownership. If they are consumed within the zone, then duty, levies and VAT become payable. If they change hands within the zone, then VAT is payable on the value at which they are exchanged. If the goods, processed or not, are shipped directly to other destinations, the free zone's hinterland does not claim duty or VAT. Only if the goods pass into the free zone's hinterland do duties and VAT become payable. A freeport will have modern docking and handling facilities, including containerisation services, areas set aside for secure and bonded warehousing and factory units for processing and assembly work.

Thus a car manufacturer may ship a consignment of components into a freeport, and lodge them in his own or an independently-owned warehouse, only calling them into his hinterland factory and paying import duty and VAT when he needs to fit them into his assembled cars. He may further decide to split the consignment and send part of it on to an assembly plant in another country and again he can do this without paying duty or VAT to the freeport's hinterland. Alternatively, he may ship a number of different components from various sources and part-assemble them in a freeport factory before shipping them out for incorporation into the final product.

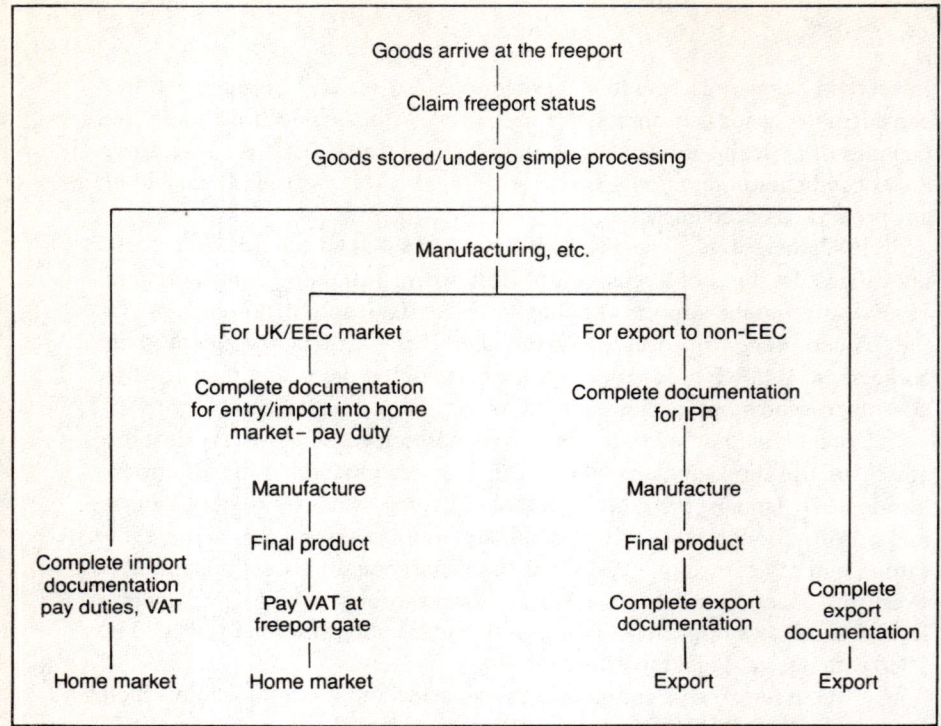

Fig. 3.1 The freeport system, Liverpool.

The flow chart in Figure 3.1, prepared by Liverpool Freeport management, illustrates clearly the options open to a freeport user. Furthermore, EEC Directive 71/235/EEC and Regulation 2763/83 list 26 processes which may be carried out in a freeport and imported across the EEC Customs border without incurring any increase in the duty that would have been paid on the goods as they entered the Freeport in their original state. These include: cleaning, conditioning, de-naturing, dividing, examining, labelling, packaging, repairing, sorting, testing, as well as processing to correct defects, greasing and anti-rust painting, decanting, mixing or drawing-off. However, if the goods are subjected to any more sophisticated processing or assembly in the free zone, then full duty, levies and VAT will have to be paid upon the value at which the goods are eventually moved into the hinterland, (which, of course, in the United Kingdom, is to any destination within the EEC). The relevant free zone procedures and documentation are detailed in section 6.4.7.

The advantages offered by free zones can be summarised as follows:

1. They can improve the price competitiveness of goods which require elementary processing or are being redistributed as part of an entrepot operation.
2. They can improve cashflow through the deferment of import charges until goods are required by the user in the hinterland or an overseas destination.
3. They can reduce administration costs because, in general, free zone procedures and documentation are greatly simplified.
4. They can improve an organisation's operating flexibility, especially if quota restraints are in force for the goods being transported.
5. They can reduce insurance costs because free zone premises are located in a high security environment.
6. They can reduce the capital costs of processing and assembling imports in cases where the free zone is nominated by the hinterland government as an area which qualifies for development grants.
7. They provide in most cases excellent communications with the hinterland, and modern handling facilities within the zone.
8. They normally have facilities for converting manually-produced documentation into their computerised equivalents which can then be used in the computer network systems which are being introduced world-wide to speed up the administrative process. (*see* section 6.4.7).

The Adam Smith Institute has produced a report on the impediments which inhibit the competitiveness of the UK freeports, in particular when compared with the freedom and advantages which are enjoyed by their continental competitors. It specifically names the following impediments to the competitiveness of UK freeports:

1. Their overseas competitors are, for purposes of levying VAT, treated as export areas. By comparison, UK freeports have to charge VAT on transactions conducted within the freeport, even if goods are re-exported without leaving the zone.
2. Overseas free zones are granted relief from excise duty whilst goods are within the zone.
3. The UK government has not done all that the EEC permits it to do to encourage inward investment by foreign companies in processing and assembly companies located within the freeports themselves.
4. There has been no authorisation for a freeport facility on the eastern and south-eastern seaboards facing the trading partners of the EEC where Britain's major growth in trade is now taking place.

4

THE REGULATION OF INTERNATIONAL TRADE

4.1 THE INSTRUMENTS OF REGULATION

4.1.1 Customs and Excise charges

Customs and Excise charges take three forms as follows:

1. *Customs duties*, which are indirect taxes levied on imports at the point of entry. The rates are laid down in the EEC Common Customs Tariff (CCT) and are standard throughout the Community. Duties can be calculated in two ways – 'ad valorem' (by value) or 'specific' (by unit measurement). They have been reduced progressively in the various GATT rounds. The full rate is now paid on imports from only a few developed countries, other countries being beneficiaries of a variety of preferential schemes. Goods can be relieved from duties in a number of ways:
   a. under EEC free circulation rules (*see* section 4.3.1.).
   b. under outward and inward processing relief procedures (*see* section 3.1.6.).
   c. under the concession which, in certain circumstances, temporarily suspends duty on some goods which are not currently produced within the EEC or are used in industrial research or for the handicapped. Further details are available from **ITP Division, Department of Trade**, Room 437, 1 Victoria Street, London SW1H 0ET (telephone: 01-215 3576).

   The new EEC members – Greece, Portugal and Spain – are still in transition to full membership. During the transition period, their exports to full member states are still subject to duty, but on a reducing scale which will render them duty-free by the end of the transition period.
2. *Excise duties*, which are also indirect taxes levied on specific products, both imported and domestically produced. The most important of these products, in terms of imports, are beers, wines, spirits, tobacco, perfume

and hydrocarbon products. Excise duties are a replacement for and not in addition to tariff duties. Currently the EEC member states have widely disparate excise duties and the European Court has ruled that these differentials have the equivalent effect to quantitative restrictions and are therefore illegal. The Council of Ministers, under guidance of the Commission, is therefore seeking to harmonise these rates, albeit slowly and reluctantly. In the meantime, goods subject to excise duties are charged with these differentials when they cross member state borders.

3. *Agricultural levies*, are charges which replace customs duties on products which are covered by the Common Agricultural Policy regime. They are adjusted annually and are highly complex (*see* section 6.4.5).

The current rates on all three forms of tax are published annually under the title *The Integrated Tariff of the United Kingdom* (*see* section 6.2.3). From the government's point of view, these three taxes have two advantages – they discourage imports and provide revenue. The weakness is that they can rarely be levied at a rate which ensures a controlled reduction in imports because of the wide range of prices at which the different exporting countries are able and willing to trade in the same product.

4.1.2 Quotas

Quotas are specific quantitative restraints imposed on the importation of nominated products. Today, they are normally applied in the implementation of trade agreements concluded between the EEC Commission on behalf of its member states and their overseas trading partners. The term 'tariff quota' is also used to describe those quantities of products which are admitted duty free or on reduced duties under the EEC generalised scheme of preferences.

The GATT lays down that, whenever quotas are introduced under its rules, they will be controlled and enforced by the exporting country, who will issue export licences which must be accepted by the importing country. The importing country is permitted to operate a surveillance scheme (often referred to as 'dual licensing') in order to monitor the effectiveness of the exporter's control machinery. However, when two countries agree to operate a voluntary restraint agreement (which is not subject to the GATT rules), then the control over quota is normally exercised by the importing country (*see* section 4.2.4). From an importer's point of view, the advantage of 'export controlled' quotas is that, because the exporter has to obtain the quota licence which guarantees acceptance at the importer's point of entry, the importer can be reasonably sure that the goods will clear UK customs. He must however exchange the export licence for a valid import licence. This procedure enables HM Customs to check that the exporting country is administering its quota system efficiently.

Under an 'import-controlled' system, the importer has to take responsibility for obtaining the necessary import licence, only perhaps to find that after he has negotiated the contract, the quota has been expended and he cannot get the goods into the country. The following product groups are subject to quota in 1987:

1. Clothing and textile products (about 80 per cent of quota products), which are subject to the Multi Fibre Arrangement.
2. Firearms and radioactive materials are subject to quotas regardless of source.
3. Raw steel is subject to quotas from all sources except EEC member states.
4. Minor quotas are applied to shoes and ceramics from certain state trading nations.

Again, the new EEC member states – Greece, Portugal and Spain – which are still in transition to full membership and whose imports were subject to quota in one form or another before they signed the Treaty of Rome, are in the process of running down those quotas progressively, so in some cases they are still in force.

In a number of special cases, quotas are actually imposed by the *exporting* country on indigenous raw materials in order to protect local industries which process those materials and thus increase the added value of their exports. For example, Egypt places quotas on its raw cotton to protect its cotton textile industry, certain South American countries place quotas on raw hides and leather to protect their footwear and leather goods industries and China places quotas on silk and cashmere yarns to protect her up-market textile and knitwear industries.

4.1.3 Currency controls

Governments frequently use currency controls of various kinds to regulate the total amount of money made available to purchase imports. Such controls are most prevalent among the state trading nations and developing countries with acute balance of payments problems. In the Peoples' Republic of China, for example, any contract signed is subject to an automatic override that hard currency will be available under the National Plan to honour it when payment becomes due. Other forms of currency control are import duty deposit schemes, which Britain has used in the not too distant past.

It is always worth an importer's while, before entering into a first contract with a new source country to check with his bank whether any such controls are in operation and, if so, how they might affect exports from that country.

4.1.4. Government subsidies

Today, virtually all governments, developed and developing, use subsidies of one kind or another to protect or render internationally competitive those of their industries which they consider to be strategically or politically important to them – steel and shipbuilding being the most commonly supported. In the United States of America in particular, government support for its high-technology arms-related industries is the main reason for its world dominance of the military hardware markets and the commercial spin-off into the associated markets for civil aircraft and computer electronics. In addition, guarantee and loan schemes of one sort or another provide barely concealed subsidies for exports and the GATT is aiming to regulate such schemes in its present Round.

The other main field where government subsidies play a significant part in distorting world trade is that of agricultural surpluses. The chief culprits are the EEC, with its provisions for dumping the surpluses of cereals and dairy products created by its Common Agricultural Policy, and the United States of America, with its support schemes for Mid-West grain farmers. The impact of this competitive dumping on the agricultural economies of the less-developed countries is, even on the most generous assessment, ill-considered. Furthermore, the erosion of commercial relations between the EEC and the United States as they compete for markets on which to dump their surpluses seriously threatens the stability of the world trading regime as a whole. What is even more distressing is that both sides are equally determined to keep the question of agriculture out of the GATT, although both have accepted that their practices will be included in the agenda for the next Round which is about to begin in Uruguay.

4.1.5 Non-tariff barriers to trade

Non-tariff barriers to trade comprise a vast range of national, unilateral regulations which prohibit the importation and sale of goods which do not conform to specifications laid down for them. Many of these regulations are justified on the grounds of public health and safety, but even so, the detail of them is all too often chosen to ensure that they act indirectly as barriers to imports. These constraints cover, among many others, food additives, units and methods of measurement, labelling, safety standards for cars, toys and electrical goods, garment flammability, exhaust pollution levels, veterinary safeguards and even calculated delays in processing customs documentation.

Both the GATT and the EEC have always accepted that these measures constitute as effective a barrier to freer trade as quotas or tariffs. However, in seeking to regulate them, the two have different objectives. The GATT wishes to control and harmonise these regulatory barriers for the benefit of international trade as a whole and proposals to achieve this have been on the table at every negotiating round. Unfortunately progress is agonisingly slow. In the EEC, the removal of such barriers is specifically included in the Treaty of Rome in Article 100. However the thrust of current EEC policy is to remove barriers to internal trade within the Common Market itself rather than with its external trading partners (*see* section 4.3.1).

4.2 THE FUNCTIONS OF THE GENERAL AGREEMENT ON TARIFFS AND TRADE

The background to and organisation of the GATT has already been described in section 1.2.4. Its influence on the activities of importers and exporters is all-pervading. The rules under which the GATT seeks to regulate world trade are enshrined in the 38 articles and nine annexes of the revised Agreement signed in March 1969. Their effects on day-to-day trading activity can be classified under five main headings:

1. the most favoured nation principle;
2. anti-dumping procedures;
3. derogations from the general principles;
4. voluntary restraint agreements;
5. The Multi Fibre Arrangement.

4.2.1 The most favoured nation principle (MFN)

This is the cornerstone of the GATT. Article II.1.a, states that 'each contracting party shall accord to the commerce of the other contracting parties treatment no less favourable than that provided for in the Schedule annexed to this Agreement'. Part I of the Schedule lists by product and territory, those items which, under MFN treatment, are exempt from duty and Part II lists the most preferential treatment in terms of duty rates which will obtain among all the contracting parties. Since the GATT was originally signed, these rates of duty have been subject to progressive reductions.

Other Articles then proceed to interpret and extend equality of treatment under the MFN principle to the following:

1. Internal taxes and charges (Article III). However, government subsidies to domestic industries are not prohibited.

THE FUNCTIONS OF THE GATT

2. Freedom of access and exemption of customs dues for 'traffic in transit' through contracting nations' territories (Article V).
3. Valuation of goods for customs purposes (Article VII).
4. Marking of goods with country of origin (Article IX).
5. Procedural charges and fees imposed on imports (Article VIII). This Article also lays down that such charges must relate directly to the cost of providing the service and that minor breaches of customs procedure and errors in documentation shall not be penalised.

4.2.2 Anti-dumping procedures

In Article VI, the Agreement lays down that dumping occurs when one country exports goods to another at less than their normal value, that is to say, when the export price is less than:

1. either that charged in the exporting country's domestic market; or
2. the highest price charged when exporting to a third country; or
3. the production cost, plus reasonable selling costs or profit margins, in the exporting country.

When dumping can be established under one or the other of these definitions, then the importing country may impose additional levies, equivalent to the shortfall in price, to the goods before applying normal tariff duties.

Article VI also distinguishes between 'anti-dumping duties' which relate to individual exporter's pricing strategies, and 'countervailing duties' which relate to price differences stemming from identifiable subsidies granted by the government of the exporting country.

To invoke anti-dumping procedures, the importing country must first produce evidence that such imports would disrupt its internal market. However, the precise definition of 'disruption' has still to be clearly established.

4.2.3 Derogations from the general principles

The Articles quoted above lay down the basis of MFN treatment in terms of tariffs and import procedures. In addition, Article XI bans the use of 'quantitive restrictions' (i.e. quotas) as a means of regulating trade. However, these general principles are subject to a number of exceptions as follows:

1. Under Article XII, countries may take measures to protect themselves against balance of payments difficulties without having to prove market disruption.

2. Under Article XVIII, less-developed countries may use protective measures to ensure the effectiveness of their economic development programmes.
3. Under Article XIX, any contracting nation may impose unilateral protectionist measures in the form of additional duties or quotas if a sudden jump in imports of a particular product threatens serious injury to its domestic producers.

In all these cases, however, any measure introduced must, under the MFN principle, be applied to imports of that product from *all* contracting parties. An importing country may not single out an individual country for protectionist treatment. Furthermore, Article XIX provides that countries which are subjected to unilateral protectionist measures under it are entitled to claim compensation by applying retaliatory measures to other products. Article XXIV goes on to interpret the provisions of the GATT in cases where contracting parties form themselves into customs unions or free trade areas.

4.2.4 Voluntary restraint agreements (VRAs)

Over the past few years, the non-discriminatory principle behind the GATT has been increasingly circumvented by a proliferation of bilateral voluntary restraint agreements. Under such arrangements, the exporting country agrees to restrict its exports of specific products to another. Because such arrangements fall outside the control of GATT, the partners are free to negotiate whatever terms they wish.

At first, these agreements tended to be imposed by developed countries, threatened by high unemployment, on the weaker developing countries. For example, such 'call-up' provisions were included in most of the EEC's Mediterranean Associate Agreements to guard against sudden disruptive surges in sensitive imports. Increasingly, however, VRAs are being used to 'arrange' trade between two developed countries. The most outstanding examples are the VRAs between Japan on the one hand and the United States and the EEC on the other concluded over high-priced consumer goods such as cars and leisure electronics.

An even more blatant VRA is that between the United States and Japan on microchips, signed in July 1986. The United States threatened Japan with anti-dumping measures if it did not agree to charge 'fair-value' prices not only to the United States but also to third countries. Japan also agreed to use its powers and influence to ensure that 20 per cent of the Japanese chip market was given to American-owned companies. Thus the world's most important new industry has been disciplined into a 'managed market' by an

American/Japanese cartel in blatant contravention of the principles of the GATT which they both signed as founder members.

Another form of VRA is the 'cartelisation' agreement under which industrialised countries agree among themselves to place ceilings on their national production to prevent price wars over the disposal of over-capacity. The best known of these are the EEC's agreed production quotas on man-made fibres and steel.

There are also private unilateral initiatives which have the same effect as bilateral VRAs. These are the products of the strategies of large multinational organisations, who seek to place specialist high-volume production units geographically on the basis of 'best-cost'. They then use their international marketing networks to distribute the outputs worldwide. In the car industry, for example, the output of these units, say gearboxes, is intra-traded between company-owned assembly units as components and the completed vehicles are distributed through various national dealer networks so that frequently these dealers will be selling a complete range of vehicles, some of which are made or assembled nationally and some of which are imported. The entire operation is a kind of 'in-company' cartel. The other industry which operates in the same multinational way is the chemical industry.

Such activities are outside the control of the GATT, Indeed even national governments are unable to influence the decisions of these multinationals to any great extent. However, it must also be said that decisions made on commercial criteria by such organisations are not necessarily more harmful than those made by governments based on emotive or political criteria.

Only the EEC has some control over these activities in that the Treaty of Rome specifically outlaws what it describes as 'abuse of dominant position', (*see* section 4.3.3). Importers who are considering joining the dealer network of a multinational organisation would be well advised to check with their trade association or the British Importers Confederation before signing anything, whether an 'abuse' action is pending or likely to arise. Even such famous brand names as Johnnie Walker's Red Label Scotch have been known to disappear without trace from certain marketplaces when the dreaded 'abuse of dominant position' is invoked.

4.2.5 The Multi-Fibre Arrangement (MFA)

The MFA is perhaps the most notorious and comprehensive example of a GATT derogation. It was first proposed and agreed because, for most emerging countries seeking to industrialise, the textile and clothing industries have been the traditional starting point. This is because the clothing industry in particular needs little initial capital investment and is labour-intensive and relatively low skilled. Furthermore, the initial target markets for low-cost production have been the fully industrialised countries with their insatiable appetites for simply designed, mass-produced garments such as knitted T-shirts, conventional shirts, blouses, trousers and jeans, and knitted garments capable of being manufactured on hand-operated machines. Unfortunately, in these markets, the domestic industries which cannot compete with the imports tend to be concentrated in a few geographical areas where they have been and still are the traditional source of its employment and wealth (such as the East Midlands in England).

Developing country after developing country has entered the same narrow markets, flooding them, initially with goods of erratic quality (which improved rapidly), at prices which the domestic industries could not compete with, thus creating further unemployment in areas which have already been exposed to the economic and social consequences of the 1973 oil crisis. As tariff barriers reduced progressively in each GATT round, they afforded less and less protection for the domestic industries of the developed countries. The result was seen statistically in what the domestic producers interpreted as alarming rises in sector market penetration – a major yardstick, in the GATT rules, for measuring 'market disruption'.

The GATT, recognising that if it failed to act the importing countries could force voluntary restraint agreements on the developing countries, accepted that the two parties concerned could negotiate between themselves 'temporary measures' to help the importing countries in their 'structural adjustment' and thus provide a climate of 'orderly marketing' in the field of textiles and clothing.

The original signatories of the MFA comprised ten developed and 24 developing countries. The ten developed countries were:

Australia	Canada	Finland	Norway	Switzerland
Austria	the EEC (on behalf of its member states)	Japan	Sweden	United States of America

The 24 developing countries were:

*Argentina	Haiti	Jamaica	Nicaragua	South Korea
*Brazil	*Hong Kong	*Macao	*Pakistan	*Sri Lanka
Colombia	(UK as negotiator)	(Portugal as negotiator)	*Philippines	Spain
Egypt	*Hungary		*Poland	Turkey
El Salvador	*India	*Malaysia	*Romania	*Yugoslavia
Guatemala	Israel	Mexico	*Singapore	

In the case of Hong Kong, this created the curious anomaly of role reversal, in that the EEC negotiated for Britain as an importing country, whilst Britain negotiated with the EEC on behalf of Hong Kong as an exporting country.

Taiwan is not recognised diplomatically and therefore was not able to sign the Arrangement. Nevertheless, it was treated by the others, for all practical purposes as though it had signed and was granted a bilateral agreement no less advantageous than those offered to the other developing countries.

Subsequently, among the developed countries, Australia and Norway, and, among the developing countries, Spain and Nicaragua withdrew. On the other hand, during the same period, the following developing countries joined:

Bangladesh	*Bulgaria	*Czechoslovakia	Indonesia	Thailand
Bolivia	China	Dominica	Peru	Uruguay

Of the developing countries which have signed the MFA itself, only those marked * have concluded bilateral agreements with the EEC.

Essentially, the text of the Arrangement was a kind of enabling framework which laid down the rules under which individual importing countries and the EEC on behalf of its members were permitted to negotiate bilateral agreements with individual exporting countries. The key provisions of the Arrangement are as follows:

1. In Article 1, the objectives are 'to achieve the expansion and liberalisation of trade' whilst acknowledging the need 'to ensure the orderly and equitable development of this trade and to avoid disruptive effects in individual markets'. These objectives were about as irreconcilable as those contained in the Balfour Declaration and could have been drafted by the same person!

2. In Article 3, importing countries are permitted to negotiate and if negotiations fail, to impose unilateral restrictions if they are able to establish that market disruption has taken place. The definition of the factors which are to be considered when establishing disruption are detailed in Annex A. The most significant of these is any substantial difference in the comparative prices of imported and domestically-produced goods of like quality.

3. In Article 4, importing countries are permitted to negotiate bilateral agreements, if they consider that there is a threat of market disruption. Under this article, the imposition of unilateral restrictions is not permitted. It is under this article and not Article 3 that the majority of the bilateral agreements at present in force have been negotiated. Such bilateral agreements must not reduce the existing levels of imports and provisions must be made for positive quota growth rates. Quotas must be administered by the exporting country through a licensing system, but importing countries are permitted to introduce a system of import surveillance in order to monitor the effectiveness of the exporter's administration.

4. In Article 6, the importing countries are enjoined to allow generous quotas and liberal growth rates in the agreements. Specifically, Annex B proposes that the minimum annual quota growth rate should be 6 per cent, but, like everything else in the Arrangement, lists two exceptions:
   a. the so-called 'Nordic' clause, which allows countries with small domestic markets to apply lower, but always positive, growth rates.
   b. the provision that if, *in exceptional cases*, clear evidence exists that a 6 per cent growth rate will cause disruption, then lower positive rates may be applied.

Despite the fact that the MFA clearly envisaged that bilateral agreements would be introduced only in 'exceptional circumstances' and as a 'temporary measure', all the developed countries made haste to negotiate comprehensive networks of them. Only Japan and Switzerland have not asked for such agreements.

The EEC lagged behind the others only because the Commission experienced great initial difficulty in drafting a negotiating mandate that was acceptable to all its member states. In the meantime, imports from the low-cost countries flooded in, raising substantially the base levels on which future growth rates would be calculated. Most of the difficulties which the EEC experienced in negotiating future extensions of the Arrangement can be traced directly to this initial delay.

Each of the importing countries developed its own standard form of bilateral agreements within the rules laid down in the basic text of the Arrangement. The form of agreement adopted by the EEC reclassified the products from the unwieldy spread in the tariff nomenclatures into, originally, 128 categories. These in turn were divided into five groups, according to their degree of 'sensitivity' (i.e. their threat to their member states' domestic industries). The result was a kind of 'quota matrix', with product categories along one axis and developing countries along the other.

Group I contained eight 'highly sensitive' products – three textile and five clothing – which between them accounted for some 60 per cent of total Community textile and clothing imports. Group II contained products assessed as 'sensitive' which between them accounted for another 20 per cent of imports. Categories III, IV and V were 'non-sensitive' and only in exceptional cases subjected to quota. Altogether, the EEC Commission eventually negotiated agreements imposing some 2,700 separate quotas, over 1,000 of which were imposed on the four newly-industrialised countries (NICs) – Hong Kong, Taiwan, South Korea and Macao. In each bilateral agreement, the product categories to be limited by quota were selected individually, according mainly to their historical market penetration levels. All quotas are expressed either by weight or unit, never by value.

Product categories not limited by quota were put 'in the basket' and subjected to surveillance by EEC member states. If surveillance indicated that imports were growing so fast as to threaten 'market disruption', then the Commission was entitled to extract the threatened product category for any particular country 'from the basket' and apply a quota to it. Hence the jargon term 'basket extractor mechanism' so frequently used by those discussing the MFA. In that this mechanism entitled importing countries to select individual countries to protect themselves against, the derogation clearly infringed the GATT rules about 'most favoured nation' treatment laid down in Articles 1 and 19.

Apart from their quota elements, the bilaterals contained the full range of other provisions laid down in Article 4 of the MFA relating to base levels, positive growth rates and so-called 'flexibility clauses' (which provided for a small degree of carry-over from one year to another and for 'swings' between categories to accommodate changes in fashion demand). The quota levels were first negotiated at Community level and subsequently rationed out (or 'burden-shared', as the jargon goes) among member states. MFA I ran from 1974 until 1977 and has since been extended as follows:

1. MFA II from 1978 to 1981;
2. MFA III from 1982 to 1986;
3. MFA IV from 1987 for a further five years.

Each successive extension was preceded by long and frequently ill-tempered exchanges which barely warranted the label 'negotiations'. The main problems were:

1. Exporters and importers each placed entirely different interpretations on what constitutes 'orderly marketing'.
2. The 1973 oil crisis slowed down demand growth in importing countries to an annual average of 2½ per cent whilst the MFA called for an annual quota growth rate of at least 6 per cent which the exporting countries tried unsuccessfully to uphold.

In all three extension negotiations, the main battlegrounds were as follows:

1. In the original 1972 MFA, in a climate of high world growth, annual growth rates for any quotas imposed were set at a minimum of 6 per cent. After the 1973 oil crisis, however, such annual growth rates would have meant unacceptably high increases in import penetration in the markets of the importing countries.
2. The importing countries felt it essential to keep the growth in imports of the eight 'highly sensitive' products in Group I as low as possible, whereas these were the very markets which the exporting countries were best able to exploit.

At each round of negotiations, the text of the MFA itself remained intact. Extension was only achieved by attaching protocols to it which had the effect of amending substantially certain parts of the original text.

In MFA II, for example, the protocol contained a provision for permitting 'reasonable departure'. This virtually tore up the growth rates originally agreed. It even allowed importing countries to impose 'negative growth rates' (i.e. cutbacks) on the four dominant newly-industrialised countries – Hong Kong, Taiwan, South Korea and Macao – with the excuse that this would enable the fully-industrialised countries to grant more generous quotas to the lesser-developed countries.

By the end of the MFA III extension in 1986, the Arrangement had, to all intents and purposes, abandoned any pretence of being a temporary expedient designed either to promote orderly marketing, or to provide growing market access for developing countries or to allow developed countries to restructure their domestic industries to accommodate such growth. It had become instead a purely protectionist measure to discriminate against and between developing countries in what were, for many, their main industrial sectors. In particular, the intention behind the cutbacks of NICs quotas (to provide more generous opportunities for the lesser developed) was never achieved. Instead, trade was diverted directly from the NICs to other EEC member states, to the undoubted disadvantage of the EEC consumer in terms of the higher prices they were forced to pay.

During 1986, the negotiations for the MFA IV renewal due to come into force on 1 January 1987, were conducted in a climate of a general world economic recovery and at first there were hopes of a certain degree of trade liberalisation. This was frustrated principally by the crisis in its trade and balance of payments of the United States of America which brought with it strong internal pressures for protectionist measures. In the end, a few, mainly cosmetic, gestures towards liberalisation were agreed:

1. The product categories were reduced from 128 to 114.
2. Growth rates were marginally more generous (particularly to those exporting countries which were having difficulties in utilising their present quotas).
3. A small proportion of children's clothing was permitted to count five garments as four adult garments.
4. A first tentative step was taken to abolish burden-sharing in favour of Community quotas on a 'first come, first served' basis.

The MFA presents the importer of textiles and clothing with two particular problems:

1. In arranging his sources, he must be particularly careful to ensure that

his supplier has, or can secure, sufficient quota licences to meet his needs.
2. The quotas create a 'sellers' market' in which the quota itself often becomes a marketable commodity. In some exporting countries, and in particular in Hong Kong, quotas can be bought and sold in the open market for fluctuating prices which reflect their scarcity value. This cost has of course to be added to the supplier's price and can vary considerably from week to week, so it is frequently impossible to predict the price at which repeat business on a particular product can be placed.

Importers should also be aware that the European Court of Justice, in its judgment 7/83 of 9 February 1974, has ruled that quota premiums do not form part of a product's price for purposes of customs valuation. Therefore it is in an importer's interest to require that the quota premium, if incurred, is shown as a separate item on his supplier's invoice and proof is produced that it has been paid. The import procedures and relevant documentation relating to products imported under the MFA regime are detailed in section 6.4.4.

4.3 SPECIAL EEC PROVISIONS

One of the most important objectives of the Treaty of Rome is to remove all obstacles to the free movement of goods, people, firms, services and capital within the European Community. In the case of goods, this is to be achieved by:
1. the elimination of customs duties between member states;
2. the establishment of a common community tariff;
3. the establishment of a common competition policy;
4. the standardisation of procedures at customs points;
5. the removal of inhibitions to free circulation within the Community by the harmonisation of any member states' laws which frustrate it.

4.3.1 Free circulation

Article 10 of the Treaty of Rome states that 'products coming from a third country shall circulate freely among member states if the import formalities have been completed and customs duties and charges having equivalent status have been levied on them.' There is still a long way to go before this ideal is achieved. At present, the main exceptions are caused by the following:
1. Different rates of excise duty and VAT in each member state. This means

that as goods pass over internal borders, adjustment payments have to be documented and paid.
2. In the case of agricultural products coming within the scope of Common Agricultural Policy, adjustment levies, called monetary compensation amounts (MCAs) are raised to compensate for fluctuations in member state exchange rates (*see* section 4.3.4).
3. The need to ensure that Community quotas which restrict the imports of certain textile and clothing products under the MFA regime (*see* 4.2.5), are shared fairly between member states. The Treaty of Rome provides that, once goods have entered the Community and all customs dues and levies have been paid on them, they may circulate freely within it. If they are subject to quota, their importation will be charged against that of the member state of first entry. If the goods subsequently move to another member state, their entry into it will circumvent any burden sharing arrangement made concerning the overall Community quota. In such circumstances, the member state whose share of the quota has been circumvented may apply, under Article 115 of the Treaty, for permission to refuse entry to the goods concerned. Article 115 was intended for use only during the initial transitional period when member states were adjusting to the new regime. The Commission has always been uneasy about using it to deal with difficulties arising from the burden sharing of quotas. Unfortunately, when it was drafted, the Treaty did not envisage that quota problems of this kind might arise. The use of Article 115 for this purpose has, however, been tested in the Court of Justice and upheld.
4. The continuing existence of a wide range of technical non-tariff barriers to trade contained in member state law.

One of the non-tariff measures most frequently resorted to by individual states are laws which regulate in some detail the composition, content, packaging and labelling of consumer products. Many of these laws have been introduced on the grounds of health and safety. The Commission has found it particularly difficult and frustrating to achieve a consensus on the harmonisation of such measures because they offer the twin attractions of both consumer and market protection.

Until, that is, the 'Cassis de Dijon' case came before the Court of Justice. Cassis is a blackcurrant liqueur made in France with a very low alcoholic content. Its traditional use had been as a 'mixer' with cheap, chilled white wine under the generic name of 'vin blanc cassis'. In the 1970s, however, as a result of skilful marketing of a brand called 'Cassis de Dijon', 'vin blanc cassis' became an international 'in-drink' under the name of 'kir' (or, mixed with champagne, 'kir royale'). A marginal, but highly profitable market for

'Cassis de Dijon' developed, among other places, in Germany. The German market makes a big thing about its food purity laws. One of them lays down a minimum alcoholic content for fruit liqueurs which is well above that contained in 'Cassis de Dijon'. The German government stopped imports of it (hoping that the German equivalent would replace it without fuss), and the importer appealed to the European Court, claiming that 'Cassis de Dijon' was not a risk to health, as it was being drunk copiously elsewhere without doing any apparent harm to anybody. Therefore, the importer argued, the law was purely protectionist and as such transgressed Article 30 of the Treaty.

The Court's judgment in this comparatively minor case has had, and will continue to have far-reaching effects on trade within the Community. It has indeed turned out to be rather more than 'a storm in a kir glass'. What the Court said can be summarised as follows:

1. Any product legally produced and sold in one member state must, in principle, be admitted to the market of any other member state.
2. Member states may only create barriers against imports where they are necessary to satisfy 'mandatory requirements' related to health, fair trading and consumer protection.
3. Any such measure must be one which attains its object with least hindrance to trade.

Not, you may say, particularly earth-shattering rulings. However, what they mean in practice is that any product which has been lawfully produced elsewhere in the Community which conforms to rules and processes of manufacture that are customary and traditional in the exporting country must be admitted to all other member states, even though it may remain illegal for domestic manufacturers to produce and sell a similar product in the country concerned, unless the importing country can establish that the product is a threat to health, safety, fair trading or consumer interests. Furthermore, whether such a threat exists is not an administrative decision; it is an issue of fact which only a court of law can decide.

Early in 1987, this ruling was applied to open the German market to British and other beers which contained additives not permitted in German brewing processes. This particular purity edict – the Bavarian 'Reinheitsgebot' dated from 1516. The judgment has also given the final death-blow to any idea of the 'Euro-product' – the legislators' dream of imposing a single European standard on all goods produced or traded within the Community.

Importers who are proposing to trade within the Community or to import products from outside the Community in the expectation of putting their products into free circulation within it, would be well-advised to investigate carefully the position regarding any new product they are thinking of introducing to make sure that none of these inhibitions to free circulation apply to it.

4.3.2 The role of harmonisation

Article 100 of the Treaty of Rome lays down that technical and legal barriers to trade shall be eliminated by 'issuing directives for the approximation of such provisions laid down by law in the member states as directly affect the ... functioning of the common market'.

The choice of the word 'approximation' implies that, before drafting such proposals, the Commission must make a comparative study of the law in each member state concerning the issue under consideration. It is then required to propose ways of 'harmonising' these existing laws so as to produce an equivalence between them. What the EEC Commision cannot do is to start with a clean slate and write completely new laws as though existing member state law does not exist. The term 'approximation' also implies that the Commission should, wherever possible, harmonise through directives, which permit each member state to accommodate the Commission's proposals in the least disruptive way. This may not necessarily be by passing new laws which merely copy the terms of the directive.

The extensive and bruising frustrations which the Commission has received during the consultative process is leading it to seek to harmonise by issuing only the broadest of guidelines, on the 'least hindrance' principle contained in the 'Cassis de Dijon' judgment. This is indeed a welcome change when contrasted with the Commission's earlier tendency to 'harmonise upwards', that is to say, to seek to introduce into all member states the most interventionist of the measures they found among them. Instead, it has largely abandoned the attempt to harmonise standards product by product in detail and will aim instead to set a basic standard concerned with safety requirements. These general standards would be compulsory and only products which met them could circulate freely within the Community.

To illustrate its ideas, the Community has drafted a model new-look directive which would cover a whole range of several dozen products. It sets out the basic requirements in terms of security, health and safety and would oblige member states to allow the importation of any product which was accompanied by a certificate of conformity to these requirements. The process of framing detailed, non-compulsory technical specifications which met these health and safety standards would be left to standardisation agencies such as the European Committee of Standardisation. The Commission intends to inaugurate this approach in three sectors: mechanical engineering, building materials (with specific regard for fireproofing), and electrical appliances.

Harmonisation legislation under Article 100 applies not only to the elimination of barriers to trade in goods and the approximation of food laws, but also to the protection of workers, pharmaceutical products, the environment, customs procedures, taxation, agriculture, public contracts, consumer protection. In 1985, the Commission produced a consultative White Paper concerning the completion of the internal market. This Paper set three objectives:

1. to bring the market together;
2. to expand it; and
3. to make it sufficiently flexible to accommodate future market changes.

It also identified a programme of specific measures (other than product specifications) which would be needed to implement these objectives, setting a target of 1992 for completing it. The programme was approved by the EEC heads of state and sponsored strongly by Britain during its 1986 presidency of the Council of Ministers.

Again, importers who are importing with the intention of putting the goods into free circulation within the Community need to be particularly careful, in the case of new products, to check on the current state of Community harmonisation legislation relating to them.

4.3.3 Competition policy

The aims of the EEC's competition policy as set out in the Treaty of Rome are 'to prevent the abuse of economic power and to induce undertakings to rationalise production and distribution and to keep abreast with technical and scientific progress'. The rules for competition laid down in the Treaty are directly applicable to member states and can be enforced by the Commission, with resort of appeal for both parties to the Court of Justice.

The Commission is torn between two courses – the pursuit of fair competition and the need for governments to ensure the viability of their strategic industries in international markets. The Commission is quite prepared to support certain types of co-operation between companies if it will increase the competitiveness of the Community's industrial base as a whole. In fact it has already accepted intervention in one form or another in the affairs of the big basic industries where there is substantial overcapacity within the Community and indeed worldwide – coal, steel, automobiles, man-made fibres, oil refining and agriculture. Such support, generally in the form of production quota-sharing or state subsidy arrangements, clearly runs contrary to the general aims of the competition policy, but the Commission has permitted their use and even participated in the negotiation of them if it is satisfied that they take the form of intra-Community agreements and are not simply designed to eliminate inter-Community competition.

Aside from these special cases, the EEC's competition policy operates in three main areas: cartels, abuse of dominant position and state aids. Cartels take a variety of forms:

1. collusion in price fixing,
2. common selling syndicates,
3. sales and production quota sharing,
4. reciprocal exclusive dealing arrangements,
5. mutual volume rebating.

These are all forbidden under Article 85 of the Treaty if they are damaging to or restrict intra-Community trade or cannot be shown to contribute to the benefit of consumers or to the promotion of technical and economic progress.

Any action by an organisation which uses its size in a market in such a way as to restrict or damage intra-Community trade by imposing unfair prices or trading conditions, limiting production, markets or technical development, or making their contracts subject to conditions which are not related directly to the subject of the contract, is deemed to be abusing its dominant position and therefore to be in contravention of Article 86 of the Treaty.

Article 92 lays down the rules and conditions under which member state governments may provide state aid to their industries and services. Here the Commission's main concern is with 'transparency', that is to say, it insists that a member state should act and inform openly and give prior notice to the Commission of its intentions. In particular, member states' aid must not create conditions of unfair competition within the Community. In its role as enforcer of competition rules, the Commission has powers to obtain access to any information it requires and can act either on its own initiative or on private complaint. It can also impose substantial fines and has frequently done so, again subject to appeal to the Court of Justice. A substantial body of case law in this field, particularly on the issue of 'abuse of dominant position' has now been built up. However, in Community law, the precedence of case law is nothing like as binding as it is in English Common Law, and Court of Justice judgments are delivered on the basis of its judges' interpretation of the Treaty provisions in relation to the evidence offered in each case.

Competition policy is of little interest to the small and medium-sized importer unless he has joined a larger organisation's dealer network. For the larger company, the Commission is increasingly inclined to the view that the achievement of a dominant position is in itself an abuse, unless it can be demonstrated beyond reasonable doubt that it is not. However, if you are large enough to be affected by the Community's competition policy, you are large enough to employ a lawyer of your own to look after such interests. For the big operator, the dangers of the doctrine of 'abuse of dominant position' are plain. Even if you do reach the top of the snakes and ladders board, there is still a long and very slippery snake lying in wait for you.

4.3.4 The Common Agricultural Policy

The CAP is covered by no less than ten Articles of the Treaty of Rome, namely Articles 38–47. Its objectives are set out in Article 39 as follows:

1. to increase agricultural productivity;
2. to ensure a fair standard of living for farmers;
3. to stabilise markets;
4. to assure availability of supplies;
5. to ensure that supplies reach consumers at reasonable prices.

This policy evolved at a time when most leading authorities were predicting that the world was about to enter an era of chronic food shortages. Europe had, for generations, relied on imports of cheap foodstuffs, much of which was capable of being produced in the temperate climate of the member states, but at a price. For this reason, it was decided to aim for as high a degree of self-sufficiency in basic foodstuffs as possible and more or less to disregard the cost of doing so.

In the 20 years since the policy was devised, some 70 per cent of the Community's budget revenues have been applied to the CAP and, in the process, the Community's self-sufficiency in agricultural products has risen from 79 per cent to 87 per cent. Yet, for all that, the Community remains a substantial net importer of food – to the extent of some £17 billion a year. Furthermore, the support which the Community affords to its agricultural sector, particularly in the form of subsidies which permit the dumping of its surpluses on the world market, has three undesirable effects.

1. It is constantly threatening to provoke a trade war with that other megadumper of agricultural products – the United States of America – which would have serious repercussions for the world economy.
2. It destabilises the social and economic structures of the poorer countries by decreasing their self-sufficiency in the agricultural sector.
3. It constitutes an unacceptable drain on the Community's resources.

Three methods are commonly used by governments for supporting their farming sectors:

1. *Subsidy schemes,* under which a government pays its farmers for not growing things.
2. *Deficiency payment schemes,* under which farmers sell their produce on the open market for what it will fetch, and the government tops up their incomes to a reasonable level.

3. *Intervention schemes*, under which a government guarantees to buy its farmers' produce at a fixed price if nobody else will and then either dump it on somebody else or store it away until somebody *does* want it.

The first of these has been used extensively by the United States (witness the well-known quotation from *Catch-22* – 'Soon he was making more money not growing alfalfa grass than any man in the country'). The second scheme was used by Britain before joining the EEC. The third scheme was selected by the six founder members of the EEC as the most appropriate means of implementing the provisions of the Treaty (as distinct from the best way of supporting agriculture!) and is still in operation.

The EEC's problem has been that, from the beginning, the scheme was open-ended, which meant that it had to pay the guaranteed price to its farmers however much they produced. This certainly concentrated the farmer's mind on modern farming methods and investment in new technology. The cumulative result of 20 years of unrelenting and vigorous pursuit of productivity improvement, can be seen today in the warehouses and silos of the Community in the shape of beef, butter and cereal 'mountains' and wine 'lakes', of sufficient depth 'to drown the Matterhorn as deep as a Mendip mine' (as Chesterton wrote about Noah's Flood).

The budget allocated to the CAP scheme has two components – a Guidance Fund and a Guarantee Fund. The Guidance Fund is relatively small and is designed to subsidise farmers in less favoured areas and to encourage the poorer and older of them to give up farming altogether. The Guarantee Fund is the cornerstone of the scheme. Each year around Christmas, the Commission has the responsibility for recommending to the Council of Ministers and the European Assembly the target prices at which it proposes to intervene in the market for all the main crops for the coming year. However, the prices themselves come into force to coincide roughly with the time of harvesting each crop. The Fund is operated by an independent organisation – FEOGA – and the process of intervention purchasing and storage is carried out by specialised agencies in each country.

The precise form which intervention takes differs from product to product.

1. *Cereals*. The intervention price is set at 7 per cent below the target price.
2. *Dairy products*. A target price is set for milk and, on that basis, differing intervention prices calculated for processed dairy products.
3. *Beef and veal*. A guide price is fixed, but intervention is paid for certain categories only and can be suspended at the Commission's discretion.
4. *Pigmeat*. The commission's powers are discretionary.
5. *Sheepmeat*. A variety of different support measures are available.

6. *Sugar* (based on the EEC beet crop, as opposed to cane imports). Price support facilities are not open ended, but subject to a complicated quota scheme.
7. *Fruit, vegetables, eggs, poultry, hops, olive oil and wine.* There are again other schemes which are not necessarily based on price support. Wine surpluses, for example, are bought in at agreed prices and distilled into industrial alcohol.

Farmers who export products in the CAP scheme are supported by payments from the Guarantee Fund sufficient to bring the price up to the Community target level. In fact, subsidies for exports, either on private initiatives or through the centralised sale of surpluses, account for approximately half of the total CAP budget.

Farmers are also protected from cheap imports by means of levies which are adjusted to ensure that the price differential between the imports' cif price and the Community target price is neutralised. Food imports which cannot be produced within the Community are excluded from the CAP scheme. They carry a small fixed duty rate which is determined under the various international agreements which the Community has concluded.

The Community's special relations network with the developing countries, its Mediterranean associates and its former dominion territories such as New Zealand provide for special treatment of various kinds for products in the CAP scheme.

As if the intervention scheme itself is not complicated enough, a further dimension is introduced by currency implications. These occur because the intervention prices are fixed in terms of the 'European currency unit' (otherwise known as the ECU), which is a weighted 'cocktail' of the national currency values. When payments are made to recipients by FEOGA, the ECU value is converted into the national currency at a fixed rate of exchange, known as the 'green rate', which can only be altered by the Council of Ministers. However, in practice, the national currencies fluctuate almost daily and so a farmer gets either less or more benefit than he should get from the subsidy. If he is trading within his own country this is just bad luck. However, when the transaction is intra-Community or export, prices are adjusted by the percentage difference between the 'green' and the 'current exchange' rates. Such adjustments are called 'monetary compensation amounts' (MCAs).

The CAP in its present 'open end' form is mainly responsible for the fact that the Community is charging lemming-like towards bankruptcy. Various attempts have been made to reform it and reduce its cost. Currently efforts are being made to 'close the end' by making intervention payable only on quotas of each product which are closer to actual Community consumption.

Despite the fact that today, no more than 4 per cent of the community's population makes its living from farming, the farm lobbies are very powerful and highly political. There is, therefore, no great consensus of enthusiasm for any of the proposed reforms. Certainly, for food importers, the CAP in its present form is the international trade's equivalent of the Grand National, with every jump a Becher's Brook. CAP procedures and documentation are discussed in detail in section 6.4.5.

PART TWO

THE PRACTICE OF IMPORTING

5

THE IMPORT TRANSACTION

5.1 TRANSACTION PRELIMINARIES

5.1.1 Types and stages of transactions

There are two basic forms in which imports can arrive in Britain – as 'goods on consignment' or as 'goods against order'.

1. *Goods on consignment* are goods which are usually consigned to an agent in the importing country with the intention that he will sell them at the best price he can obtain and then take commission on the sale. The goods remain the property of the consignor until they are sold to the agent's customer.
2. *Goods against order* are goods despatched by an overseas exporter in response to instructions received from an importer.

Before an importer enters into an arrangement to do business with a new overseas supplier, he is well advised to check carefully into that supplier's credentials. In fact, if he has not already done so, a check on his existing sources may well throw up some surprises. How creditworthy is he? The reply will give some guidance at least about the prospect of him remaining solvent for long enough to meet his obligations. How big is his operation? What are his main markets? Who else is he supplying in the United Kingdom? How reliable is he in terms of quality control and delivery performance? Is there a history of problems with the type of merchandise he is proposing to supply (caused either by factors in his country which are beyond his control or by the sourcing of his raw materials)? All these are pointers to the exporter's potential efficiency and his ability to deliver the right goods at the right time.

A typical import transaction will divide into the following stages:

1. Placing the order.
2. Transportation and documentation procedures.
3. Entry and customs clearance.
4. Delivery to destination.

5. Fixing the selling price.

It is also advisable, at the earliest possible stage, to decide on the strategy for getting the goods from the supplier's factory to the point of use or sale.

To assist all parties involved in stages 2 to 4, the International Chamber of Commerce (ICC) has produced a *Guide to Incoterms No. 354* which explains in detail the different 'Terms of reference'. The Guide provides full explanations of the various 'shorthand' terms used in international trade to describe the division of responsibilities between supplier, carrier and importer. It can be obtained from the **International Chamber of Commerce**, Centre Point, 103 New Oxford Street, London WC1A 1QB, but most chambers of commerce will hold a library copy of the Guide. A summary of these terms is shown at Appendix A.

This range of choice allows the importer a high degree of flexibility in determining the most competitive means of transporting goods from the overseas factory to the point of use or consumption. Generally speaking, and subject to satisfactory arrangements for payment, the title to the goods passes to the importer when the foreign supplier has discharged the appropriate set of responsibilities which he has contracted to perform.

5.1.2 The order

In any transaction, the critical stage is the actual placing of the order for the goods, if only because this placement involves the importer in accepting certain commitments which will generally be enforceable in law. First, therefore, a public health warning. An importer should never enter into a commitment to do business with a new source or in a new product without first consulting a legal adviser experienced in trading law. If he has not done so with his existing arrangements, then it would also be wise to go back and do the same with them.

The conclusion of a successful negotiation will almost certainly end in some sort of agreement to trade, either verbal or written. For an agreement to become a binding and enforceable contract it must give both parties rights and liabilities which the law can recognise. There are two basic forms of contract:

1. A 'simple' contract, which does not necessarily have to be written down to be enforceable, although, if it is not, then there needs to be some clear evidence that it exists.
2. A 'specialty' contract made under seal which must be written and delivered, but this type is almost never used in trading arrangements. If a supplier as much as mentions the possibility, an importer needs to take legal advice as fast as possible.

However, 'simple' contracts *for sale of goods* are also governed by the Sale of Goods Act 1979 which defines 'goods' and 'a contract for the sale of goods' in fairly straightforward terms and lays down the implied rights of the seller and the protection afforded to the buyer. For a 'simple' contract to be valid and enforceable it has to meet the following requirements:

1. The transaction must contain the three elements of offer, acceptance and consideration. All three words, for this purpose, have special technical meanings.
2. The parties must be capable in law of performing their contracts. Do not appoint as your import manager a 15-year-old Youth Opportunity Scheme secondee, even if he speaks 15 languages fluently.
3. The substance of the contract to be performed must be legal.
4. There must be an absence of fraud or mutual mistake.

Of these conditions, that of offer, acceptance and consideration is the one which is most frequently misunderstood.

Either party to a transaction may make an offer to the other. 'Acceptance' means that *all* the terms in an offer are accepted without amendment. If the other party wishes to amend the terms offered, then his amended terms become the 'offer'. The process of offer and counter-offer forms the negotiation of the contract. When the final terms are agreed, then those terms become the contract, the party who finally proposes them becomes the 'offerer' and the other party the 'accepter'. Thus two of the elements of a binding contract have been fulfilled. In practice, when negotiations occur, it can be difficult to distinguish between the offer and the acceptance.

The final element of a 'simple' contract – 'consideration' – is, in contracts relating to the sale of goods, something of a legal nicety, the role it performs being akin to that performed by the Holy Spirit in the Christian Trinity. It is legally defined as 'some real and future interest, profit or benefit accruing to one party and some forbearance, detriment or loss of responsibility given, suffered or undertaken by the other'. More simply, it can be regarded as a 'value', so that, for example, gifts are not contracts, because they lack 'consideration'. For all intents and purposes, the element of 'consideration' in a sale of goods transaction is satisfied by the promise of one party to sell and of the other to buy, the goods concerned at an agreed price.

The law of contract in other countries may differ in a number of respects from that of the United Kingdom. It follows that, in placing an order with an overseas supplier, an importer would be well advised to exercise great care and precision when drafting its terms and conditions as, through them, the order may well acquire the status of a contract. The following, therefore, are some of the main ground rules which an importer needs to follow when placing an order with a new supplier for the first time:

1. Because the law of contract may differ from country to country, it should be agreed in writing which country's laws will apply when interpreting the terms and conditions of the order.
2. Time and expense can be avoided by including an arbitration clause as part of the terms and conditions. This clause should specify that both parties will accept a settlement of any dispute which might arise from a specified arbitrator. Favoured arbitrators for this purpose are the International Chamber of Commerce, the London Chamber of Commerce and the London Court of Arbitrators. Some countries, however, have overriding laws which stipulate that foreign law cannot take precedence over local legislation and that any disputes arising on commercial contracts when one of their nationals is party to it, must be settled there.
3. Because problems can arise over language interpretations, even when parallel texts have been prepared by experienced, authorised translators, the terms and conditions should state clearly which of the two translations is the definitive master copy for all legal purposes.
4. If the importer intends to establish a longer-term relationship with the supplier, then he should consider drawing up a preliminary written agreement which outlines the common principles which will govern the terms and conditions of doing business. It would then only be necessary to make reference to these principles on subsequent orders.
5. Whenever possible the importer should, from the beginning, take the initiative in drawing up and offering the terms and conditions on which he wishes to do business and should make every effort to secure the signature of the other party to them. It should also be remembered that, if 'unaccepted' terms and conditions are altered during negotiations, the party which produces the finally-accepted draft is deemed to be making the offer.
6. The conditions should contain a provision that goods supplied must conform to the appropriate requirements of the UK Health and Safety laws.
7. The importer should include provision for the inspection of the goods before he accepts responsibility for their being transferred to him. Again, considerable time and expense can be saved if this inspection is carried out before it leaves the exporter's country. It is worth noting that many overseas Chambers of Commerce now offer this facility of independent inspection to overseas customers. Details can be obtained from the **British National Committee, International Chamber of Commerce**, Centre Point, 103 New Oxford Street, London WC1A 1QB (telephone: 01-240 5558). A Certificate of Inspection should include the following information:

a. identification details of packages containing the goods inspected;
b. results of qualitative or analytical examinations of samples;
c. shipping details.

5.1.3 Terms and conditions

In drafting the terms and conditions of an order for new business, it is necessary to cover as many as possible of the contingencies that can be foreseen. These should include the following:

1. A clear definition (including, if necessary a technical specification) of the goods being purchased.
2. The quantity being purchased.
3. The price to be charged, together with any other charges and discounts agreed during negotiation.
4. Method of packaging and transportation to be used.
5. Place and time of delivery.
6. Settlement terms and method of payment.
7. Other rights and responsibilities of the two parties concerned.
8. Terms for settling any claims which might arise.
9. Which country's law will govern the contract.
10. Arbitration procedures.

Terms and conditions which govern the placing of foreign trade orders have become reasonably standardised. Here again, the International Chamber of Commerce has prepared a brochure which defines the commonly-used terms and conditions in some detail. It is always advisable for an importer to obtain from his supplier a detailed making specification for the product he is proposing to purchase and, if possible, a definitive sample. In fact, a good practice is to obtain two samples, check them against the specification and return one to the supplier 'sealed' as a token of the standard expected.

Today, the majority of large retail organisations practise a system of 'specification buying' under which they themselves lay down in detailed manufacturing terms what they wish to buy from their suppliers. Certainly there is every reason for even a smaller importer to expect to participate actively in the technical specification of what he proposes to buy rather than accept without comment what the supplier wishes to make. An order is deemed to have been fulfilled when the terms and conditions of the order have been met, goods have been delivered either to the purchaser or his nominated agent and the purchaser has paid for them. The responsibility for the condition of the goods and for insuring them remains with the vendor until he has met the terms and conditions of the particular 'Incoterms' agreement between them (*see* Appendix A).

5.1.4 Settlement terms and payments

An important element of the terms and conditions of an order for goods is the arrangement for payment. The choice will depend to a great extent on the exporter's ability and willingness to offer credit and is, in any case, inextricably linked to the 'terms of trade' (*see* Appendix A). The problem that arises is how to arrange payment terms which reconcile the reluctance of the exporter to part with his goods before receiving his money, with the equal reluctance of the importer to part with his money before receiving the goods. Manifestly, the critical point in the transaction is the moment at which the exporter is deemed to have fulfilled his contractual obligations. From the importer's point of view therefore, the longer he can postpone this moment the better off he is in financial terms. Equally however, the longer it is postponed the longer it is before he has control of the costs of importing. The selection from the 'Incoterm' arrangements listed in Appendix A is therefore very important to him.

Another issue is the selection of the currency in which the transaction is to be conducted. If the contract runs for a lengthy period, currency fluctuations could well wipe out a large part of the importer's profit from it. Much of this uncertainty can be removed, either by buying currency forward at stable rates, or by selecting a stable neutral currency. This issue is discussed in more detail in section 7.2.2.

The supplier will almost certainly try for some form of cash in advance – either with order or in the form of substantial advance deposits. If the manufacturing cycle is a lengthy one, then he might ask for progress payments against work completed. If an importer is forced to agree to such terms, he should at least require a guarantee from the supplier's bank that it will refund any advance in full if the terms of the contract are not fulfilled. The options for cash settlement are cheque, banker's draft, telegraphic transfer, international payment or money order. The importer would naturally prefer to treat the import transaction on a normal domestic basis and pay monthly after delivery. Not surprisingly, the overseas supplier's enthusiasm for this arrangement is minimal. However, if he operates through a local subsidiary or an agent this might well be arranged, but it will almost certainly be reflected in a higher price.

Because of this conflict of interest, the most common practice is to use some facility which employs an intermediary such as a bank, which will make payment only when evidence of performance is produced. Such facilities take two main forms: a bill of exchange or a letter of credit. The essential difference between the two facilities is that, in the case of a bill of exchange, the bank is looking after the interests of the exporter, whereas, in the case of the letter of credit, it is the importer whose interests the bank is protecting.

A documentary bill of exchange (otherwise known as cash against documents) is governed, in the United Kingdom by the Bills of Exchange Act 1882. It takes the form of a demand by the foreign supplier for payment. He will draw up this demand on a formal printed document and send it to his own bank together with all the supporting documents which prove performance of the contract on his part. His bank will then send the bill of exchange together with the supporting documents to a bank in the United Kingdom which will arrange to collect it. This bank will release the documents to the importer and thus enable him to take possession of the goods when he has paid in the required sum on the date nominated on the bill of exchange.

The legal definition of a bill of exchange is that it must be an unconditional instruction in writing which is:

1. addressed from the 'drawer' (i.e. the exporter) in person to the 'drawee' (i.e. the importer or his bank) also in person;
2. signed by the drawer; and
3. requires the 'drawee' to pay on the nominated date a certain sum of money to the order of a 'payee' (normally the exporter himself).

There are two alternative forms of bills of exchange:

1. Documents against payment (DP) which means that the importer pays before the documents are released to him.
2. Documents against acceptance (DA) which means that the importer accepts the documents and signs a bill of exchange drawn on him which is to be met at a given future date.

As the exporter is responsible for remittance charges, he must give precise instructions as to how the money is to be remitted.

A documentary letter of credit is a formal undertaking given in writing by a bank to an exporter on behalf of the importer to pay for the goods providing that the exporter complies precisely with the terms and conditions in the letter. Its object is to substitute the credit of a well-known bank for that of a less well-known trader. From an importer's point of view, it means that his money will not be paid over until documentary evidence has been produced to his bank that the stipulated conditions have been fulfilled. To enable a letter of credit to be issued, the importer must make arrangements with his bank for the necessary funds to be available to ensure that the letter can be met. Such funds may take the form either of a separate facility for each letter or of a revolving credit facility which covers any number of letters up to a specific ceiling value. There are three types of letter of credit.

1. *A revocable letter* which permits the importer to instruct his bank to revoke it at any time before payment is due. Such a letter requires a high degree of trust between the two contracting parties and is therefore rarely used.

2. *An irrevocable letter* which, once raised, cannot be revoked under any circumstances, so once performance is completed, the money is as good as in the exporter's bank.
3. *A confirmed irrevocable letter* which provides both belt and braces for the exporter in that a bank in his country agrees to pay promptly if the importer's bank does not do so, but of course at the price of two commissions instead of one.

The important point about a letter of credit is that the issuing bank is on the side of the importer and will only pay up if all the conditions contained in the letter are met. These conditions will contain a list of all the documents which the bank needs in order to establish that the exporter has fulfilled his obligations under the contract of sale.

A recent study carried out by the Simplification of International Trade Procedures Board (SITPRO) reported that some 52 per cent of letters of credit were rejected on first presentation because of failures to complete them properly. They attributed this lamentable state of affairs to the lack of formal training facilities in import procedures, to a lack of management control and to poor communication. They identified the main reasons for rejection as being discrepancies in transport documentation and invoices, late presentation and elementary spelling mistakes which are not acceptable in documents of such precision. To assist with this problem, SITPRO, with its project 'Data Interchange in Shipping' (DISH) is co-operating with banks and carriers in the setting up of an electronic communications link between the main participants in international trade. SITPRO has also produced a series of 'Letter of Credit Checklists' which can be obtained from **SITPRO**, Freepost, London SW1Y 6BR. Further information in the form of two booklets *Uniform Rules for Collection* and *A Standard Code of Practice on Documentary Credits* on both bills of exchange and letters of credit can be obtained from **British National Committee, International Chamber of Commerce**, 103 New Oxford Street, London WC1A 1QB (telephone: 01-240 5558). Once again, however, any importer contemplating a long-term trading relationship with a new overseas supplier should seek expert advice from his bank at an early stage in the negotiations and not leave the initiative of proposing settlement terms to the exporting supplier.

5.2 MISCELLANEOUS ISSUES

5.2.1 Samples

Samples serve two main purposes: to solicit orders ahead of the arrival of the main consignment of goods and, to act as a means of ensuring that the goods are of agreed quality and specification. The first of these uses is the most common. In the second case, because of the problem of language and communication, perhaps the most satisfactory way for an importer to ensure that he is getting the goods he *thinks* he has agreed to buy is for him to obtain and hold a specification sample. Earlier it was further suggested that he should obtain two samples, check that they are identical and satisfactory, then return one to the supplier 'sealed' as a token of his acceptance of the standard and quality he is expecting. This practice would be particularly useful if the importer decides to have the goods inspected by an independent body before they leave the exporting country, because the manufacturer's sealed sample can be used by that body.

In most cases, the overseas manufacturer will provide both types of sample free of charge. However, HM Customs will not automatically exempt them from duty or VAT. In fact they can only escape these two imposts if they are deemed to be either 'of negligible value' or 'a facility for purposes of demonstration'. In the case of 'goods of negligible value', Customs normally require that they be defaced either by tearing or by indelible marking. Clearly, this is not much use if the samples are to become a selling aid, but could be used as a way of avoiding duty and VAT on specification samples.

In the case of 'a facility for purposes of demonstration', Customs Notice 105 sets out details of arrangements for the temporary importation of samples without payment of duty or VAT providing:

1. they are owned abroad;
2. there is a firm intent to re-export them;
3. they can be clearly identified at the time of re-exportation;
4. they are imported free of charge;
5. they are used solely to demonstrate the product;
6. deposits to cover duty and VAT are lodged with HM Customs.

This temporary importation facility is designed for high-priced capital goods rather than normal consumer goods. For consumer goods, there appears little alternative to paying duty and VAT on samples which are not defaced. If however, the temporary importation facility can be used by an importer, he should, of course, take out adequate insurance cover for the transaction.

5.2.2 Aftersales servicing arrangements

Today, an increasing range of goods can only be marketed if they are backed with an effective warranty, repair and servicing arrangements which normally form an integral part of the offer from the trader to the consumer. In any case, in the United Kingdom, consumers have certain implied rights regardless of whether or not they are included in the terms and conditions set by the trader in his offer and these rights cannot be set aside by so excluding them. For example, under the terms of the 'Supply of Goods (Implied Terms) Act 1973, goods must be of 'merchantable quality'.

Over and above 'implied warranties' are warranties which offer additional security and services to the purchaser and these are covered by the Sale of Goods Acts 1893 and 1979. Such warranties need very careful drafting and so, once again, it is advisable for an importer not to accept such warranties from a new overseas supplier without first having them checked by an expert. If there is, in the terms and conditions of the offer to sell to the consumer, an undertaking to replace or repair faulty goods, then the importer must accept responsibility for providing and administering such services. He will also have to face the problem of deciding whether claims from consumers are good or false.

Frequently too, there are problems with any servicing manual which the supplier produces. It may not be available in English at all or perhaps even worse, may be written in English which is barely recognisable and certainly incomprehensible. Many a media programme or article on consumer affairs would be dull stuff without resort to frequent quotations from them, especially those which purport to be assembly instructions. As somebody once remarked about such an instruction sheet: 'They claim it can be put together by a five-year-old child, but unfortunately they don't supply the child.'

Manifestly, an importer, faced with a warranty situation, must make arrangements either to obtain access to a facility for tracing faults and repairing goods which are returned to him, or to maintain a sufficient stock of replacement goods to offer a rapid replacement service. The importer's best hope is that his supplier has already established a repair and replacement facility in the country in order to support other UK customers. If not, then the importer could consult the appropriate trade association in order to find a suitable technical service organisation which is prepared to undertake the work under contract. Only as a very last resort should he consider setting up such a facility of his own from scratch. The alternative, of holding merchandise in stock to provide simply a replacement service, requires the careful framing of that part of the agreement with his supplier which refers to the return of faulty merchandise. Here again, the best procedure to use for the return and replacement of such goods is the outward processing relief system (*see* section 3.4.2). In this case, the procedure needs to be initiated by the UK importer, using Customs and Excise Form 1173 to apply for the procedure and Form 1152 to re-import replacement or repaired goods. Customs Notice 235 (Nov. 1985) describes the procedures to be adopted.

Needless to say, all these eventualities need to be taken into consideration when pricing the product and estimating them in terms of possible unit cost requires very careful judgement.

5.2.3 Product pricing

Once upon a time, a buyer, faced with a suggestion from his supplier that he should pay more because manufacturing costs had risen is said to have replied: 'What on earth has cost got to do with price?' Well, at least from an importer's point of view, everything.

There are two main pricing strategies open to any trader. The first, and probably the most commonly adopted, seeks to minimise the cost price by negotiation and close product specification, to apply the lowest possible mark-up and so seek to maximise profits by generating a high turnover. The second strategy seeks to find a product for which the consumer is prepared to pay a premium price, establish the highest selling price the market will bear and to produce the item to a precise *market* specification with little regard for cost. Then, once the market has been established and consolidated, to seek to reduce progressively the production costs through a process of 'product engineering' without altering the nature and market appeal of the product and without necessarily passing on the benefit of such reductions to the customer.

Certainly there is no reason why an importer should automatically apply a set mark-up to the calculated cost price of his goods. There is nothing immoral about handsome profits if they are a reward for marketing skills and judgement and there are plenty of opportunities about for exploiting carefully designed and merchandised products which are not price-sensitive. High mark-ups only make a trader vulnerable to competition if effective *price* competition really exists. Nor is there any reason why a trader should not mix these strategies in his range of offers if the market will stand it. Any demand by a buyer to do business on the basis of an open costing book should be steadfastly resisted. An importer who wishes to do business with one of the large retail organisations who operate 'specification buying' policies might have to make this concession, but of course there are costing books and costing books.

However, whatever pricing strategy an importer may decide upon, the *first* stage in producing a price list is accurate costing. The basic stages of product pricing are as follows:

1. *The unit manufactured price* will almost certainly fluctuate according to the manufacturer's input prices for labour and raw materials and so much will depend on the stability of the exporting country's economy. In any case, it is a subject which the manufacturer might well be unwilling to discuss, unless he wishes to place conditions on his offer which relate to such costs.
2. *The ex-works price* will provide some room for manoeuvre in negotiation and will probably depend on the size of the order which the importer is

prepared to place. If he does not wish to place a substantial and firm initial order, then it might be worth his while for him to explore the possibility of fixing a price for doing agreed levels of future business in accordance with a planned take-off programme, on the understanding that a firm repeat order against such a plan will depend on sales experience. Although he may not get the same attractive price which is on offer for a large firm contract, the prospect of future continuity could be a useful negotiating ploy.
3. *The landed and delivered prices* can be used by an importer as reference points for making decisions about which form of transportation he should select and whether or not he should use his own forwarding agent.

It is perfectly reasonable, in the negotiating stages, to ask a supplier to prepare alternative quotations for ex-works, landed and delivered options in addition to the more traditional CIF and FOB quotes. If asked to provide a range of quotations, an exporter would usually make a firm ex-works offer and give a provisional estimate of the 'add-ons'. The offer from the exporter may take a number of forms:

1. a standard price list;
2. a simple letter quoting prices and terms;
3. a tender for a specific one-off contract; or
4. a pro forma invoice.

The advantage of the pro forma invoice is that, if it is accepted by the importer as it stands, it can be used to obtain import licences in advance of receipt of the formal invoice. All quotations should include a guaranteed delivery date. An offer will be one of two sorts – conditional or unconditional. A conditional offer is only binding on acceptance and is subject to price fluctuations and time limits: an unconditional offer is not and so is preferable.

The currency in which the order is to be transacted is of vital importance and should, of course, be provided for unequivocally in the terms and conditions negotiated. Whatever is agreed, however, in reality the following costs will be incurred in the currency of the exporter:

1. Manufacturer's production and overhead costs.
2. Packing costs.
3. Docks charges at port of exit.
4. Insurance to point of hand-over of responsibility.
5. Outward bound consular charges.
6. Export documentation charges.
7. Any agent's or other commission paid by either party in the exporter's country.

The following costs will be incurred in the currency of the importer:

1. Customs duties.
2. Landing, warehousing and transportation costs in entry country.
3. Any agent's commission paid by either party in the United Kingdom.

The currency in which the remaining costs must be paid, namely: freighting, shipping charges (including administration and documentation) and insurance from point of arrival will depend upon the terms and conditions of the contract of sale, the point at which the importer takes over responsibility and whether or not he decides to use a forwarding agent.

Finally, an importer should exercise very careful judgement in allocating his overhead costs to final unit prices. The rule is simple. Allocate them rationally if possible, otherwise allocate them arbitrarily, but make sure to allocate them *all*.

5.2.4 Requirements of exporting countries

Many exporting countries have a variety of special rules, even about their outward trade. Many such rules are related to their policy concerning, and needs for foreign currency. Some, for instance, require to see evidence of a firm order from an overseas customer before they will release currency to their manufacturers to purchase the necessary imported raw materials or components. Others have strict rules about which currency is to be used in foreign transactions. Some insist that, regardless of what agreement is reached among the parties, only their own law can be used to interpret it. Others are keen to explore every possibility for countertrade or joint commercial ventures before accepting a more straightforward transaction involving the direct exchange of goods for money (*see* section 3.4.3).

Some require that their exporting manufacturers produce a 'delivery verification certificate' from their overseas customers, confirming that the goods have been delivered to their proper destination. If these are requested, they can be obtained by the importer from HM Customs and Excise after he has completed Form C598 and lodged it with Customs and Excise when presenting his Customs Entry Form.

Obviously, therefore, when doing business with a new country or in a new product, an importer should take care to ask his potential supplier about such conditions and incorporate them in the terms of the agreement between them. If the exporter does ask for such provisions, the importer should, as a matter of routine, check them out with the appropriate foreign consulate or section of the DTI before agreeing to them, in order to make sure they really are necessary.

5.2.5 Health, safety, and consumer protection

Apart from the body of legislation which regulates the flow of external trade, importers are required to conform to another body of law which requires that their traded goods meet certain standards concerning health, safety and consumer protection.

The overriding requirement placed on a trader by the Sale of Goods Act 1979 is that the goods he offers for sale are of 'merchantable quality and fit for normal use'. It is the responsibility of the importer to ensure that whatever he imports and offers for sale meets, not only this basic requirement, but also conforms to a whole range of other standards laid down in a labyrinth of legislation. Indeed, trading in goods today is a trader's nightmare and a lawyer's dream. The body of recent legislation is partly a codification and up-date of UK law as it stands and partly an adaptation of it to conform to directives and regulations imposed on it by the European Commission's drive to implement the provisions of the Treaty of Rome (*see* sections 1.2.5 and 4.3).

The laws relating to health and safety as they affect goods offered for sale are, for the most part, embodied in the following Acts of Parliament:

1. The Medicines Act 1969.
2. The Agricultural Act 1970.
3. The Poisons Act 1972.
4. The Consumer Safety Act 1978.
5. The Food Act 1984.
6. The Telecommunications Act 1984.
7. The Weights and Measures Act 1985.

These, quite properly, regulate the content and labelling of merchandise in the interests of the users' health and safety. Even so, although the concept of health and safety is fairly straightforward, the practical day-to-day implementation of it is fraught with difficulties.

For example, anything added to natural foodstuffs is viewed with varying degrees of suspicion both by career health-watchers and the public at large. Properly, there are stringent laws about what can and cannot be added and about disseminating information concerning these additives on the labelling. However, some medical authorities would argue that many of the additives, especially those designed to prolong the life of the product, have made many of our foodstuffs less rather than more dangerous to consume and have thus increased rather than harmed our general health. Again, the gases given off by ignited synthetic foam padding used in, for example furniture can be lethal in seconds, but an absolute ban on their use could increase the price of furniture beyond the means of many families.

Finally, it is manifest that certain toys are highly dangerous to children. But, take a construction set. The small pieces which could be dangerous to a three year old who tries to eat them are an intrinsic part of the attraction of the toy for a 13 year old. Clearly it would stultify the toy trade if *all* toys had to be made safe for three year olds, so some form of classification of danger needs to be incorporated into the labelling. But what happens if a family has both a three and a 13 year old?

Health and safety regulations are therefore an understandable battleground for legislators and traders; most of the answers they eventually find are compromises which are open to criticism by lobbyists of all persuasions. The technical details of standards which have been agreed are set out in the form of guidelines by the **British Standards Institution** and can be obtained in pamphlet form from their offices at 2 Part Street, London W1A 2BI.

The Consumer Safety (Amendment) Act 1986 gives Customs the right to detain any goods until their safety has been established. It is therefore advisable for an importer to require, as part of the terms and conditions of the order he places, that the overseas supplier produces a certificate from an authorised testing house stating that these requirements have been met before delivery is accepted. Such a certificate should show:

1. details which clearly identify the consignment;
2. results of any qualitative or analytical tests which have been conducted; and
3. shipping details.

If this is not possible, then the importer is well advised to submit a sample of the goods concerned to a UK testing house before the goods are offered for sale in this country.

The laws relating to other forms of consumer protection are embodied in the Trade Descriptions Acts 1968 and 1972 and, the Consumer Protection Act 1987. Between them these Acts:

1. prohibit the use of false or misleading descriptions;
2. make it a criminal offence for manufacturers or importers to sell unsafe goods;
3. make it a criminal offence to give consumers misleading price indications;
4. introduce no-fault product liability; and
5. allow the defence that the goods offered comply with BSI and similar standards.

Again it is advisable for the importer to protect himself as far as possible by including the requirement to conform to these laws in the terms and conditions of his order. (A list of approved BSI standards is available in the DTI library, 1 Victoria Street, London SW1.)

5.2.6 Trading Standards officers

In the United Kingdom, the laws relating to health, safety and consumer protection are enforced by Trading Standards officers, who belong to a department of local government which evolved from the former Weights and Measures inspectorate.

Trading Standards officers do the following jobs:

1. Inspect shops, markets, factories and importers' premises.
2. Take samples for testing.
3. Maintain a watch on advertisements and product labels.
4. Investigate complaints from both consumers and traders.
5. Verify measuring equipment.

Their responsibilities include not only protecting consumers from traders but also traders from each other.

Originally their main duty was to detect offences and, where necessary, prosecute offenders but today they are more concerned with preventing offences, particularly those resulting from misunderstandings and misinterpretations. To this end, they are always prepared, and indeed anxious, to discuss possible problems with traders providing the will to remedy faults exists, and they can be very helpful, understanding and flexible when thus consulted. Many importers have developed the practice of consulting with their TSOs about all new merchandise they are considering offering for sale and this can be warmly recommended to all.

Deliberate fraud is of course another matter altogether: the majority of offences created under these protectionist laws are classed as criminal acts and carry substantial penalties.

6

IMPORT ENTRY PROCEDURES

6.1 HM CUSTOMS LEGAL INSTRUMENTS

6.1.1 Customs legal requirements

HM Customs and Excise are regulated by the Customs Consolidation Act 1876, (amended annually as necessary by the Finance Acts), and Special Acts which, since the UK entry into the European Community in 1972, ratify trade agreements and legislation already adopted by the Council of Ministers. On the basis of these Acts, information about duties to be paid and preferential treatment accorded to certain products and trading partners are published annually in *The Integrated Tariff of the United Kingdom*. This contains information concerning the following:

1. The classification of products.
2. Rates of duty to be levied.
3. Tariff preferences.
4. Relief from duties.
5. Prohibitions and restictions on imported goods.
6. Procedures for and completion of customs entry documents.
7. Information about computerisation of customs records and procedures.
8. Customs transit codes.

The Tariff is discussed in more detail in section 6.1.3.

The day-to-day procedures followed by HM Customs and Excise are governed by regulations issued under the Import of Goods (Control) Order 1954. This lays down that Customs and Excise is responsible for:

1. Collecting all charges, duties, VAT and other levies to which imported goods are liable on entry into the United Kingdom.
2. Controlling goods subject to health and quarantine restrictions.
3. Maintaining a statistical record of UK and EEC trade.
4. Preventing the importation of prohibited goods.

The basic legal requirement is that all goods which enter the country must be cleared through an authorised Customs entry point (which is normally a sea or airport). Failure to meet this requirement is a criminal offence, regardless of whether or not the goods concerned are prohibited or liable to duty. These entry points are organised for administrative purposes into 22 geographical 'Collections', each administered by a Collector (*see* section 2.2.2).

Details of imported goods must be entered on the relevant customs entry form and accompanied by the appropriate set of documents and these must be presented to the Customs Office before the goods are removed from the place of entry. If goods have arrived by land or sea, the documents must be presented between four days before or 14 days after arrival of goods; if by air, within seven days of arrival. If the entry forms cannot be completed within these times, application may be made, under indemnity, for release of the goods, giving name and address of importer, location of consignment and identification details of the goods, on the understanding that entry details will follow by an agreed date.

All goods are liable to examination by Customs but, in practice, only between 5 and 8 per cent are checked in detail. The importer must arrange for the goods which the customs officials wish to examine to be unpacked. Then, if the entry procedures are in order, the Customs Office releases the goods for internal circulation within the United Kingdom and, in fact, in most cases, within the EEC also.

6.1.2 The import licence

Under the Import of Goods (Control Order) Regulation 1951 goods can only enter the United Kingdom under a licence to do so. Licences take a number of forms as follows:

1. *An open general import licence (OGIL)* which was issued by the Department of Trade and Industry in November 1983. It permits entry, without further licensing formalities, of all goods except those listed in Schedules 1 and 2 of OGIL Order No. 15 1983 or those which are the subject of a special licence. The customs entry form is itself an application to import goods under this licence.
2. *An individual import licence* for goods listed in the two schedules, which can be either:
    a. An open individual licence which permits the holder to import the commodity specified on it without limit as to quantity, value or source; or
    b. A specific individual licence which sets limits on quantity or value to be imported from a specific source.

Either of these can be obtained from **The Import Licensing Branch, The Department of Trade**, 375 Kensington High Street, London W14 8QH (telephone: 01-603 4644).
3. *A surveillance licence* which requires the goods to be named or defined but sets no limit on quantity or value. These licences are used in cases where, under an international agreement, quotas may be imposed if there is a sudden, disruptive increase in imports of the products concerned.
4. *Special licences* are issued against application in the case of Multi-Fibre Arrangement clothing or textile categories and certain steel products both of which are subject to quotas. Such quotas must, under GATT rules, be administered and issued by the exporting country, with import licences being issued by the importing country automatically on production of the export licence. This dual licensing system is used by the UK Customs solely in order to monitor that the quotas are being properly controlled by the exporting country. Applications for these import licences must be made on Form ILB/W which is available from **The Import Licensing Branch, Department of Trade and Industry**, Ebury Bridge House, 2-8 Ebury Bridge Road, London SW1W 8QD. The application for such licences must be supported by:
   a. clear evidence of a firm intention to import the goods in the form of a contract, an order or a letter of intent, and
   b. a valid export certificate from the exporting country, where applicable.

Licences also have to be obtained for certain agricultural products where entry is conditional on their having been treated in certain ways before exportation. Licences and further details can be obtained from: **The Intervention Board of Agricultural Products**, Fountain House, 2 Queen's Walk, Reading RG1 7QW. For licensing purposes, the world is divided by Customs and Excise into nine areas and coded accordingly. These divisions accord roughly with a set of common procedures and documentation which relate to a specific trading agreement or regime. The CTC codes for individual countries which are required on the Single Administrative Document (C88) are listed in Appendix C1 of Customs Notice 484 (July 1987) or, alternatively, in Appendix E of *The Integrated Tariff of the UK*.

6.1.3 The Tariff

The Tariff is the importer's bible. It is the prime source for the essential information which is needed to perform the function and complete the procedures of international trading. In Britain, the custodian of the Tariff is HM Customs and Excise, which publish it annually under the title *The Integrated Tariff of the United Kingdom* which can be purchased from any HM Stationery Office. It is in loose-leaf form, binders are available and the price includes an update amendment service.

HM Customs also issues procedural working manuals in the form of customs notices and amendment slips which can be obtained free from local customs offices. They are summarised in the *List of Customs and Excise Notices*, which are published in the DTI's weekly magazine *British Business* and in the publications of most trade associations which cater for importers as they are issued. These customs notices are of vital importance to importers as they provide the latest definitive information about every aspect of customs procedures. It is particularly necessary to watch for amendments to them. A consolidated list of these customs notices is shown in *The Integrated Tariff*, Volume I, Part 15.

The Integrated Tariff breaks down all traded goods by commodity into a number of separate classes, specifying, in each case, details of duty and levies to be charged and any preferences which are available. In practice, the network of exemptions and other preferences is now so extensive that only the leading industrialised countries – the United States of America, Canada, Japan, Australia, New Zealand and South Africa – and some of the Eastern European state trading nations pay the full rate of duty.

Although the importer himself is responsible for classifying his goods according to the Tariff, HM Customs and Excise are the final arbiter on classification. If the importer gets it wrong inadvertently, clearance can be substantially delayed; if he gets it wrong particularly with the intention of evading the full duty, then penalties are severe. To assist the importer to classify their more difficult products, Customs issues a number of *Special Guides*, the most important of which is probably No. 12 – *Textile Apparel*. These guides can be obtained from **The Customs Directorate**, Div. C7, Dorset House, Stamford Street, London SE1 9PE (telephone: 01-928 6533, ext. 2217).

As a member of the EEC, Britain is subject to the Common Customs Tariff (CCT), This is administered by the Community's Customs Service, which is an integral part of the EEC Commission in Brussels. The CCT quotes two rates of duty:

1. *The autonomous rate*, which is the rate before the reductions negotiated under the GATT rounds have been applied and can, for all practical purposes, be ignored.
2. *The conventional rate*, which is the rate after the GATT reductions have been applied.

HM Customs and Tariff quotes only the conventional rate because, under the 'most favoured nation' rule, that is the rate which is charged, even to non-GATT countries.

Tariff classification is also used as the basis for the production and presentation of world trade statistics exchanged between trading nations. These statistics are an important factor in the international negotiation of trade agreements and are used frequently to support demands for more national protection. The rules for tariff classification are drawn up under international conventions.

Before 1 January 1988, the Brussels Tariff Nomenclature (BTN) was based on the Customs Co-operation Council Nomenclature coding system (CCCN) which was used for classifying only about half of the world's trade. The United States of America, Japan and Canada, among others, used different codes. The CCCN system was based on a four-digit code (or more accurately, on two pairs of numbers separated by a full stop). The first figure of the code represented the 'Division' and the first pair of numbers represented the 'Chapter'. The EEC's Brussels Tariff Nomenclature (BTN) attached two further digits, separated from the CCCN number by a dash. These two digits catered for the Community's tariff and statistical needs and was known as the NIMEXE 1982 code. The United Kingdom's Tariff Trade Code Number (TTCN) attached a further two digits, again for UK statistical purposes, making eight digits in all and this was the basis of the code numbers quoted in *The Integrated Tariff of the United Kingdom* ('The Tariff'). Each Tariff classification showed also the form and level of tariff and excise duties and agricultural charges (which replace duties under the EEC's Common Agricultural Policy provisions). For further details of the CAP *see* section 4.3.4.

The CCCN was drawn up over 30 years ago and, although it has been frequently revised, it became increasingly inadequate to deal with the new 'high-tech' sectors and the arcane needs of the Common Agricultural Policy. It was also designed exclusively for Customs purposes, with little regard for the other commercial uses which require trade to be classified. These deficiencies have become increasingly manifest as integrated and interactive computer systems have come into service. Consequently, a new international coding system was developed known as the Harmonised Commodity Description and Coding System (HS) and this came into operation on 1 January 1988. Countries which account for over 90 per cent of world trade are transferring to HS, including, for the first time, the United States of America, Canada and Japan. The move to HS is described in section 6.2.2, along with the other major changes in internal trading procedures known collectively as Customs 88.

6.2 CUSTOMS 88

6.2.1 General introduction

The introduction of widespread changes in import procedures which are the end-result of 12 years of international negotiations within the Customs Co-operation Council took place on 1 January 1988. The changes, which are designed to rationalise and, it is hoped, simplify the administration of external trade worldwide, are known collectively as Customs 88. The changes subsumed into Customs 88 are, in reality, the consequence of three separate initiatives:

1. An *international* initiative to harmonise the classification of goods for tariff purposes.
2. A *European Community* initiative designed to improve the procedures of Community intra-trade in order to make free circulation a reality.
3. A *United Kingdom* initiative to replace the present computer system with one more compatible with modern international trading requirements.

The four changes which, taken together, have major consequences for UK importers from January 1988 were therefore as follows:

1. The introduction of a new international Harmonised Commodity Description and Coding System (HS) designed to meet the present-day needs of all aspects of international trading.
2. A new European Community Integrated Customs Tariff (TARIC), based on the HS classification which will combine the present Common Customs Tariff (CCT) and the Community's statistical classification system (NIMEXE). *The Integrated Tariff of the United Kingdom* is based on TARIC.
3. The introduction into the European Community of a multi-purpose single administrative document (SAD) which will be common to all member states and replace, as far as possible, the present proliferation of Customs Declaration and Community Transit documents.
4. The introduction into the United Kingdom of a new computer system known as 'Customs Handling of Import and Export Freight' system (CHIEF) to ensure a better interface with other international computer systems. It will be based on HS, TARIC and the SAD and is designed to encourage a more widespread use of computers in clearance and transit transactions.

Each of these changes is dealt with in turn in the sections which follow.

6.2.2 The Harmonised Commodity Description and Coding System (HS)

HS is the replacement, at the international level, of the present Customs

Co-operation Council Nomenclature (CCCN) which has been in operation for the past 30 years. Several countries are joining the system for the first time, including the United States of America, Canada and Japan, which means that it will govern virtually all trading transactions worldwide.

Under the HS system, the current 99 two-digit 'chapters' have been reduced to 96 and some have been reorganised. However, for the majority of goods, the classification codes are perhaps deceptively similar. Although the number of chapters has been reduced, the current eight-digit code will be replaced by a nine-digit code for use in intra-Community trade and an 11-digit code for use in trade with non-Community countries. In addition, a further four digits have been added for a limited number of special import situations arising under the Common Agricultural Policy.

The overall result is that the European Community classification now breaks down into 5,000 six-digit headings, compared with the more rigid 1,000 headings under the old four-digit code. The trade-off for this apparent regression into further fragmentation will be seen in the Integrated Customs Tariff (TARIC, *see* section 6.2.3), where it will now be possible to show all the necessary Customs information for each product description on a single line, instead of, as under the previous Tariff, having to resort to appendices and footnotes for certain facts. The HS is also suitable for a wide range of other classifications, such as freight tariffs, where, previously, some 13 other independent classification systems were in operation.

When HS was introduced on 1 January 1988, all existing classifications of goods had to be changed and it was the responsibility of the importer to determine the new classifications for all imports presented for clearance after that date. To assist in this process, HM Customs has produced a guide to reclassification – *CDC 100* – which can be obtained free of charge from any Customs or HM Stationery Office. To assist further in this changeover, HMSO has published a book of *Correlation Tables* alongside the new 1988 Tariff. This lists the 1987 CCCN codes in terms of the 1988 HS codes by reference numbers only. It is not a definitive correlation. Only some 50 per cent of the new classification descriptions are exact analogues of the old, so importers are advised, when seeking to classify goods they know under the old classification, to check the actual description of goods under the new tariff once they have looked up the new code number in the *Correlation Tables*. These *Tables*, at the end of each of the chapters, also list the codes which have moved in and out of each chapter in the changeover. The *Correlation Tables* can be obtained from: **HMSO Books**, POB 276, London SW8 5DT, quoting the reference ISBN 011 983824. More detailed explanatory notes of the HS nomenclature are also available from HMSO at a price of £150.

6.2.3 The Integrated Customs Tariff (TARIC)

TARIC is the European Community's new Common External Tariff which is based on the HS classification described in section 6.2.2 above. The problems of the current Tariff have already been discussed in section 6.1.3. The United Kingdom's national version of it is called *The Integrated Tariff of the United Kingdom* and comprises three volumes:

Volume 1. General information.
Volume 2. Schedule of duty and trade statistical descriptions, codes and rates.
Volume 3. Customs freight procedures.

The companion volume to the tariff is that containing the *Correlation Tables*, which are designed to assist in the reclassification of the 1987 Tariff in terms of 1988. This has already been described in section 6.2.2 above. TARIC has three objectives:

1. To bring together on the same page of the Tariff all details relating to the importation of goods.
2. To enable the introduction of more sophisticated computerised entry procedures.
3. To allow all essential tariff data to be transferred by electronic means between EEC customs authorities, traders and importers.

The information contained in *The Integrated Tariff of the United Kingdom* comprises duty and excise rates, agricultural levies, preferences, quotas, duty suspensions, import licensing, surveillance and protective measures and countervailing duties. A specimen page, illustrating the new format, is shown as Appendix C.

HMSO is also planning to offer, as an alternative to the tariff book, a magnetic tape package at a price of £150 plus VAT. This can be ordered from **New Media Section, Publication Division HMSO**, St Crispins, Duke Street, Norwich NR3 1PD (telephone: Norwich (0603) 695550). At the time of writing, only Volumes 1 and 3 together with the *Correlation Tables* have been published. Volume 2, which contains fine detail concerning the tariff, is awaiting the outcome of GATT negotiations to ensure that any changes in duty rates caused by reclassification will be adequately neutralised across the board.

Volume 1 contains the following sections

1. Introduction.
2. EEC and accession of new members.
3. Import prohibitions and restrictions.

4. Export prohibitions and restrictions.
5. Common Agricultural Policy.
6. Anti-dumping and countervailing duties.
7. Preferences.
8. Tariff quotas and ceilings.
9. Suspension of customs duty.
10. Reliefs from duty and VAT.
11. End-use relief.
12. Excise duties, reliefs and drawback.
13. VAT and car tax.
14. Valuation.
15. Notices.
16. Appeals.
17. Explanation of abbreviations and terms.

Much of the drafting of this volume is a significant improvement on that of previous tariffs; in particular, section 6 on anti-dumping and countervailing duties and section 14 on valuation are admirably clear. Section 17, a glossary of abbreviations and their meaning is also very helpful.

In the main, the administrative procedures laid down for 1988 show very little change from those of 1987 and before; the main procedural changes relate to documentation and this is dealt with in Volume 3 and in the next section of this book.

6.2.4 The single administrative document (SAD)

The single administrative document (SAD) is the brainchild of the European Community's Customs Union and has been some 12 years in gestation. It has, for the Customs Union been something of a Holy Grail. Under the present system, when goods move between member states, it is necessary for declarations to be made at both departure and arrival, and much of the information provided on each entry is identical. In concept, therefore, the SAD has been designed not only to eliminate this duplication, but also to replace some 70 separate forms, 27 of which, listed in Appendix F of Volume 3 of *The Tariff*, are in frequent use. By introducing the SAD, the amount of information which importers or agents need to provide for Customs will be halved.

In practice, of course, the replacement of the multiplicity of special-purpose forms by a single comprehensive form has not been achieved without some sacrifice. The SAD is complicated, but, as the Duke of Wellington observed about war, designing documents for such a complex operation as external trade is 'an option of difficulties'. The original concept has had to be modified in a number of ways:

1. Existing simplified procedures such as Period Entry will continue to operate in their present form.
2. Provisions have been made for the import, transit and export functions of the document to be separated (the 'split-use' or 'salami' option, so-called because it permits the single sausage to be sliced into more convenient portions). This will accommodate the present pre-lodgement facility used extensively by forwarding agents.
3. Certain additional documents which cannot be readily accommodated on the SAD, principally those for supporting CAP export refund claims and administering drawback, have been retained.

The multi-purpose function of the SAD has been achieved by requiring that only certain boxes of the SAD will have to be completed for each of the functions it performs. A useful summary of which boxes have to be completed in each function it performs is shown in Appendix B of the *Customs 88 Information Note No. 5* (March 1987). In reality, therefore, the SAD is capable of being used in a number of different procedural roles from a single flexible format. The advantage of this is that information common to the different functions is only recorded once, and this is the real saving. Another advantage is that, whichever of the uses the SAD is put to, it remains a single document format for purposes of computer input punching and output printing.

It has also been found possible to produce a modification of the basic SAD by adding a number of boxes to accommodate details of duty payments, so that it can also be used for trade with non-EEC countries. The only difference now is that imports from EEC member states will be identified by a nine-digit classification code number, whereas imports from other countries will require the 11-digit code (nine of which will of course be the same). This classification code number will be entered on the SAD in box 33, which has accommodation for 22 digits. The code numbers for the short and long codes will be entered in positions 1–9 and 1–11 respectively. However the additional four digits used for special CAP purposes referred to in section 6.2.2 will be entered in positions 15–18, which means that positions 12–14 and 19–22 must be left blank.

The uniformity of SAD usage will be further increased by the convention which has now been signed between EFTA and the EEC which ensures that, for Customs 88 purposes, EFTA members will be treated as though they are members of the EEC.

But, all this having been said, the SAD document itself is complicated to use. In its basic form, the SAD – now to be known officially as C88 – will consist of eight copies on self-copying paper:

Copies 1–3 – the export function, with copy 1 replacing copy 1 of the T

Form, copy 2 being used for export statistical purposes and copy 3 being the exporter/agent's copy.

Copies 4–5 – the transit function with copy 4 replacing copy 2 of the T Form and copy 5 replacing copy 3 of the T form.

Copies 6–8 – the import function with copy 6 replacing the present Customs Entry Form, copy 7 being used for import statistical purposes and copy 8 being the importer's copy.

Copies 1–3 are identical, as are copies 6–8.

The SAD is also flexible enough to accommodate a number of variations in operational practice:

1. Traders using computerised entry systems may use plain paper, providing they design the printer output to conform to the standard screen display format laid down by Customs.
2. Traders whose computer printers cannot cope with eight copies at once in a single set can use instead two four-part sets, by re-numbering the second set as follows:

    copy 1 becomes copy 6
    copy 2 becomes copy 7
    copy 3 becomes copy 8
    copy 4 becomes copy 5

Pre-printed SADs, already made up into four- and eight-part sets, as well as other special-purpose sets to accommodate facilities such as 'option-splitting' (see above), are available from Customs. A specimen of the basic SAD (C88) is shown as Appendix D.

When the SAD is used to import goods from non-Community countries, importers may be required to show their calculations of value on a separate form. If computerised CIE procedures are used, then a new 'Value Build-up Sheet' (C89) must be used in conjunction with the SAD. A specimen of this new form is attached as Appendix B to Customs Information Note No. 6.

A further feature of the SAD is the extent to which standard codes are used for completing the boxes on the form. This will help to a significant extent to overcome the language problems inherent in any multilingual system. These box codes are described in Customs Notice 484 (July 1987) in Section 4 of the Introduction and listed in Section 3.4.1 and in Appendices C, C1, C7 and E. This Notice is in effect a free copy of Volume 3 of *The Tariff*, which describes the procedures to be followed when completing the various transit and clearance formalities. It is laid out as follows:

Section 1 General information.
Section 2 Exports and Community transit outwards.

Section 3 Imports and Community transit inwards.
Section 4 Entry for removal to Customs warehousing regime.
Appendix A Specimens of the various versions of the C88 Form (SAD).
Appendix B Describes which boxes copy through in order to convert the four-part to the eight part set.
Appendix C The box codes which have already been agreed.
Appendix D Commentary on relevant Customs Notes.
Appendix E Lists the new Customs procedure codes (CPCs) which replace the present Customs transaction codes (CTCs).
Appendix F Lists the most frequently used forms the SAD replaces.

Appendix F, is reproduced, by permission of HMSO, as Appendix E to this book. Clearly, the most important of these sections is Section 3 – Imports and Community transit inwards. The content of its sub-sections is as follows:

3.1.	Provides detailed notes for completion of the SAD boxes for all the most important procedures.
3.2.	Deals with the simplified procedure for import clearance of low-value consignments (SPIC).
3.3.	Deals with period entry procedures.
3.4.	Deals with local input control (LIC), inland clearance depots, inter-part removals, postal imports, temporary imports and TIR carnets.
3.5.	Deals with Customs and Excise warehousing, free zones and re-imports.
3.6.	Deals with Community transport procedures.
3.7.	Deals with Common Agricultural Policy goods.
3.8.	Lists documents providing special information not included on the SAD which, if required by Customs, must accompany it. In particular:
3,8,14	Lays down the conditions under which telex or facsimile documents can be accepted in place of the originals.

It is important to appreciate that, in general, it is not the old *procedures* which have changed, only the forms used to initiate and implement them. Furthermore, these changes in documentation only involve the substitution of the SAD (C88) or elements of it, for a substantial number of the documents in use up to January 1988.

6.2.5 The Customs handling of import and export freight (CHIEF)

The computerisation of customs procedures and records in the United Kingdom started in the early 1970s when the airlines, freight agents and

HM Customs co-operated in the development of a system for direct trader input (DTI) for Heathrow Airport called LACES. Later in the 1970s, the system was adapted for use at the larger maritime ports to form the current UK system known as the 'departmental entry processing system' (DEPS).

DEPS has worked well enough but is based on out-of-date computer programs which make changes to the system difficult and expensive, especially those designed to promote an interface information exchange with the systems in other countries with whom the United Kingdom trades extensively. UK Customs are therefore introducing a new system called the 'Customs handling of import and export freight' (CHIEF). It is being designed from the start to operate the new Customs 88 procedures. The European Commission has long-term plans to introduce an integrated system to be called 'Co-operation in the automation of data and documentation for imports/exports and the financial control and management of the agricultural markets'. Happily, all this is known familiarly as CADDIA. CHIEF is also being designed to interface with this system, as well as those in other major trading countries.

The present system for period entry (*see* section 6.4.1) will be amended to accommodate HS and the SAD but will otherwise continue to operate in parallel alongside CHIEF. HM Customs has had dialogues with both the suppliers of software packages and with traders who use computers, in an attempt to ensure that the programs are altered to accommodate Customs 88. At the time of writing, HM Customs has announced that they have had to defer work on CHIEF because of the pressures of HS and the SAD. They now expect to begin the introduction of CHIEF sometime at the beginning of 1990.

6.2.6 The importer and the introduction of Customs 88

During 1987 HM Customs went to great pains to educate and inform traders and agents about the changes and how they will affect 'life after 88', in the following way:

1. They provided a series of free *Information Notes* (the latest being No. 60, which are in effect progress reports. Any importer who is not on the mailing list for these notes can apply to be included on it to **Customs 88 Project, HM Customs and Excise**, Room 301 Dorset House, Stamford Street, London SE1 9PS.
2. They promoted a series of awareness seminars throughout the country in association with SITPRO, the Freight Transport Association and the Institute of Freight Forwarders. They also actively support similar training sessions run by the CBI, the Association of Chambers of Commerce and the British Importers Confederation. In addition, these

organisations prepare their own 'distance learning packages' for in-house training.
3. They appointed to each of the Collections a special 'Customs 88 Liaison Officer' who is available to answer queries and speak at local functions on demand and appointed also to each Collection a 'Classification Officer' to assist traders with their reclassification problems. These Liaison and Classification Officers are listed in an Appendix to *Information Note No. 6*. Alternatively, importers can be put in touch with them through their local customs office.

The steps, therefore, that an importer should have taken to implement Customs 88 are as follows:

1. Ensured that he is aware of the new HS code numbers and descriptions of the goods in which he is dealing. (HM Customs will not do the job for him, but might be persuaded to check borderline cases. However to assist in this process of reclassification, HM Customs has produced pamphlet CDC 100 *Classifying your imports* which can be obtained from **HM Customs and Excise**, Customs Division C, Dorset House, Stamford Street, London SE1 9PS.)
2. Ordered into stock supplies of the new forms in the correct part sets when they become available.
3. Checked which documents will be replaced by the SAD (C88) form, into which boxes the entries transferred from the old forms will go, and which are the appropriate box codes to be used.
4. Checked which additional documents will be needed to support the SAD for the operations in which he is involved.
5. Checked with his Community suppliers and agents that the new documents will be available for all shipments received after 1 January 1988. (And hope that they are all as well informed about the changeover as he is.)
6. Checked that his non-EEC suppliers and agents will also produce the new documents for shipments after 1 January 1988 (because if not, the importer will have to transcribe the details from the old forms to the SAD before submitting them to Customs).
7. Checked that any computer software package he uses for import purposes has been adapted to handle HS and SAD information and that his operators are adequately trained to operate them.
8. Made sure that he knows the name and telephone number of his nearest Customs 88 Liaison Officer.

He might also consider producing an in-house 'import procedures guide' of his own which extracts all the relevant information and instructions about the products in which he trades and the sources he uses. He will almost certainly receive help and encouragement from his Customs 88 Liaison Officer in such a project.

6.3 TRANSPORTATION AND INSURANCE

6.3.1 Freight handling and transportation

A substantial proportion of the final cost of imported goods results from the need to move them from one country to another. The administration and routing of these movements is complex and the techniques are in a permanent state of modernisation and rationalisation. The three main agents of change have been the standardised container (and the allied development of the special container ships and roll-on-roll-off ferries), the jumbo-type freight aircraft, and computers, which are playing an increasing role in improving the efficiency of the raising and transfer of trading documents. Here again, the field is so specialised that an importer needs the services of an expert. If his operation is extensive enough to justify the employment of a freight manager then all well and good. If not, then he should consider using the services of a freight forwarding agent (*see* section 3.5.2).

Even so, if he is to get the best from either choice, an importer should be sufficiently informed about the processes and options involved to negotiate with and make judgements about the expert he decides to employ. This section therefore concentrates on the general background to freighting and shipment operations.

By far the most important managerial function which any importer needs to perform is to set up and maintain an effective monitoring and progress chasing system of his own, even if the actual functions are performed by others. Such a system should be co-ordinated with the process of initiating and checking of all the freight and customs documentation which relates to it.

An importer who has agreed with his supplier the terms of transportation (selected from the options offered in the list of Incoterms summarised in Appendix A) and decides to use a forwarding agent should be aware of the following:

1. Goods can be transported by sea as 'open' cargo, by sealed standardised container, or on a goods vehicle which can drive on board.
2. Alternatively, they can be transported by road or rail in a conventional 'open' goods vehicle or rail van or in a sealed container or vehicle.
3. Containers can travel by road on an articulated trailer, by rail or by a combination of the two, transhipment normally taking place at a selected rail container terminal.
4. Groupage is available on any of these means of transport through a forwarding agent (*see* section 3.5.2)

5. Goods can enter the United Kingdom through ports with computerised facilities which significantly speed up clearance (*see* section 6.4.1).
6. 'Open' loads need to comply with customs procedures at each border crossing they use, whereas 'sealed' loads can travel to the point of entry to their final destination without having to comply with intermediate formalities. In the case of 'sealed' loads, the seal is applied at the point of departure and its number recorded on the vehicle transit documents. On arrival at the point of entry, Customs may or may not inspect the seal to ensure that it remains unbroken. On arrival at its destination, the importer should check that the seal is intact, because a broken seal may affect any claims concerning the condition or content of the consignment.

The use of sealed containers and vehicles (henceforth referred to as 'container/vehicle'), is now so widespread that it is the subject of special clearance procedures. To be accepted for these procedures containers/vehicles must be approved and certified by the Department of Transport as conforming to certain standards. They must fulfil the following conditions:

1. Be sufficiently enclosed to provide a compartment to hold the goods.
2. Be easy to load and unload.
3. Contain no concealed spaces where goods can be hidden.
4. Be readily accessible for customs inspection.
5. Have provisions for affixing seals simply and effectively.
6. Bear unique identification marks.

In the case of containers, they must also:

1. Be strong enough for repeated use.
2. Be designed to carry goods by one or more forms of transport without intermediate reloading.
3. Be easy to handle at depots and between modes of transport.
4. Have an internal volume of not less than one cubic metre.

Because airfreight containers cannot comply with these specifications, goods transported in them may still qualify for these special procedures if they are offloaded from the plane into a sealed container which does.

Heavy or bulky goods which cannot fit into a container or sealed van and goods carried on sealed train/ferry wagons may still qualify for these special procedures if certain conditions laid down in Customs Notices 309 and 464 are met.

Containers, whether domestically or foreign owned, have to be accounted for as though they were themselves traded goods and must be entered and cleared under simplified procedures. All container charges must be included when valuing goods for duty. Seals are of two kinds: traders' seals; customs' seals.

Traders seals may be affixed by the consignor and broken by the importer at an approved place without a Customs Officer being present.

Customs seals may only be affixed by Customs and broken in the presence of or under clear authority from a Customs Officer.

The sealing of containers/vehicles enables such vehicles:

1. To pass unhindered through countries other than those of departure and destination under TIR procedures. The Transport International Routier (TIR) regime is designed to facilitate the passage of 'sealed' consignments across the borders of countries through which they pass on their way to their final destination. It is governed by the Customs Convention on the international transport of goods under cover of TIR carnets 1975. The Convention goes into great detail over the definition of containers, vehicle types and dimensions, liability guarantees, transport procedures for both normal and abnormal loads and the issuing of the TIR carnets themselves. Once the conditions and requirements of the Convention have been met, customs officials *en route* are obliged to accept the customs seals or other identifying marks affixed to the load without further inspection formalities. A vehicle operating under the TIR Convention must carry a square plate bearing the initials TIR. A TIR carnet is valid for one journey only. Full details of this system are set out in Customs Notice No. 464.

2. To pass through points of entry into the country of destination without necessarily conforming to point of entry customs clearance procedures. Once entry has been formally registered, the containers/vehicles can move directly either to an inland clearance depot (under inland clearance procedures) or to the importer's premises (under local import procedures). Inland clearance procedures are set out in Customs Notices 464 and 464A and local import procedures in Customs Notice 309. Details of documentation are set out in Customs Notice 484 (July 1987) describing the use of the Single Administrative Document. The relevant sections are 3.4.1 and 3.4.2

Inland clearance centres in the United Kingdom are listed in Appendix B. Arrangements are available, under both procedures, for forwarding agent's consolidated loads imported in sealed containers/vehicles to be broken at the point of entry under Customs supervision for detailed distribution and for them to be resealed for transportation to, and clearance of the remainder at, their final destination. The procedures and documentation of such operations are set out in Customs Notice 484 (July 1987) in section 3.4.3.

In the main, the administrative systems for transporting and clearing freight have been built around shipment by sea, but shipment by air, road and rail are of growing importance and, for each, significantly different procedures have been developed.

Shipment by sea is still the most economical and reliable method of moving goods over long distances in bulk, especially for British importers. The development of the standardised freight container has resulted in the extensive modernisation of Britain's major ports to handle them. A number now have specially designed container terminals within their old boundaries, which has improved almost beyond recognition the efficiency and speed at which cargoes are handled and ships turned round. Three of the UK ports – Liverpool, Southampton and Cardiff – have their container terminals located within their new freeport enclaves (*see* section 3.5.3).

Shipment by sea involves the importer in another special form of contract with his exporter, and the ship (or shipping agent) called a bill of lading, which is governed by the Bill of Lading Act 1855. The bill of lading performs a number of functions as follows:

1. It acts as a receipt for the goods when it is transferred from the possession of the exporter and certifies that they have been received in good condition and are properly packed, that is to say, they have a 'clean bill'.
2. It serves as a promise from the shipper to deliver the goods in the same condition to the consignee.
3. It acts as the title to the goods which needs to be produced as evidence of ownership before the goods are handed over to the consignee.
4. It describes in great detail the duties of the carrier (and particularly, which risks he does not take). These conditions were translated into a standard international code known as the Hague Rules of 1921.

Normally two or three original copies are raised and these are known as the negotiable copies, because possession of them imputes title. For purely administrative purposes, other non-negotiable copies may be raised.

In the United Kingdom, transactions by bill of lading are governed by the Carriage of Goods by Sea Act 1924, (which, in effect, ratified the Hague Rules and the subsequent Hague-Visby amendments made to them in later years).

If delivery to final destination involves more than one method of transport, then a 'transportation bill' is also raised, which allows reshipment to take place beyond the point of discharge of the ship by the means nominated on it. If a forwarding agent is consolidating consignments from more than one exporter destined for a number of different importers, then he raises a 'group bill', a copy of which goes to each consignee to enable him to obtain the goods without the need for the common bill of lading (which continues to be held by the shipping agent).

The usual practice is for consignors to pay transportation charges in advance against a 'freight note' in which case the bill of lading is endorsed 'freight paid'. Sea freight charges are calculated either by ton weight or by volume displacement (measured in cubic metres), the latter being the most prevalent mode. 'Conference rates' are those agreed by a cartel of shipping lines and are designed to attract regular bulk business to them.

Shipment by air was transformed by the introduction of the jumbo-type freight aircraft in the 1970s and by the adaptation of containerisation systems for use in them; this increased significantly the range and volume of goods which could be shipped economically by this means. The main advantages of air freight are as follows:

1. Packaging costs are appreciably lower, because less handling is involved.
2. There is a lower risk of damage and pilferage.
3. Insurance costs are lower, because of the shorter transit times involved.
4. It provides opportunities for a faster and more flexible stock turn and customer servicing facilities.

Unlike sea freight, rates are based on a *combination* of weight and volume – one rate for consignments of 45 kilos or below, another rate above 45 kilos, with the two rates being applied on a sliding scale based on units of 550 cubic inches outside Europe and 427 cubic inches within it.

As with sea freight, freight forwarders practise grouping and consolidation and pass the benefits on to their users, and there is normally a concession called a 'commodity rate' on regular bulk shipments. Together, these can save up to 25 per cent on standard rates. The goods are consigned on an air waybill raised by the freight forwarder which also acts as his receipt to the consignor. It is not a document of title and travels with the goods on the aircraft; in all other respects it performs the function of a bill of lading. All the other documents which are required to support a bill of lading are also required to support an air waybill, but, in many respects, documentation for air freight is simpler than for sea freight.

Shipment by road is probably the most flexible and economical of the options, for all but bulk goods. With the introduction of roll-on-roll-off (Ro-Ro) ferries, it is the most practicable route from Europe.

The problems of road transport are mainly those of the carrier or forwarding agent rather than of the importer who uses his services (unless of course, the importer decides to run his own transport operation). If he does, then he should first read Largent Brown's recently-published *A Manager's*

Guide to International Road Freighting (Kogan Page 1986) which describes in detail the procedures and problems which he will face).

In the case of the road system, something very similar to the old Mercantile Act is in force, which regulates the number and nationality of lorries permitted to operate across international borders and controls strictly the type, size, construction and weight limits of vehicles and operating conditions for drivers. For every journey across frontiers, a lorry needs an individual permit, the conditions for which are laid down in the International Road Haulage Permits Act 1975. All operations are governed by the Convention on the contract for the international carriage of goods by road (CMR).

Furthermore, to ensure that the lorries themselves are not being permanently imported and evading duty and taxes, each lorry has to carry a 'carnet de passage en douane' which is used by border authorities to ensure that vehicles which enter a country also leave it. There are, in many countries also, rules which limit the amount of duty-free fuel which any lorry can take across the border in his tank. There are additional procedures to be completed for the movement of 'abnormal loads' as follows:

1. Loads which are of 'extraordinary dimension, shape or weight' require special routing and prior negotiation with the appropriate traffic authorities.
2. Loads consisting of dangerous substances are regulated by the European agreement on the international carriage of dangerous goods by road (ARD). A special booklet called *A Guide to the Classification, Packaging and Labelling of Dangerous Substances Regulation 1984* is available from the **Health and Safety Executive**, Room 414, St Hugh's House, Stanley Precinct, Bootle L20 3QY.
3. Perishable commodities have to be moved in containers or vehicles which meet the conditions laid down in the international agreement for carriage of perishable foodstuffs (ATP). Today, an important requirement is to maintain the 'cold-chain' so that goods do not unknowingly defrost and refreeze during transit. The International Carriage of Perishable Foodstuffs Regulation 1985 lays down which foodstuffs come under the ATP and maintained temperatures at which they must be transported. The fact that this temperature has not been exceeded during transit should always be checked by the importer on the instrument provided on the vehicle.

Shipment by rail is subject to special simplified procedures for two main reasons:

1. Virtually all incoming rail freight arrives from EEC or EFTA countries,

the procedures for which follow those of the Community transit system laid out in Customs Notices 750 and 751.
2. The railways have formed jointly an organisation called Intercontainer Societé Cooperative based in Switzerland which specialises in moving containerised goods by rail. It is represented in the United Kingdom by Freightliners Ltd and Cory Brothers of Felixstowe.

The simplified procedures for import clearance of goods by rail (SPIC) are set out in CN 753 and in section 3.2 of Notice 484 (July 1987) – *the Single Administrative Document.*

6.3.2 Risks and insurance

Risk insurance is a highly specialised subject, which again requires expert guidance. This is available either from a forwarding agent or directly from an insurance broker who specialises in trade risk cover. Although the details are complicated, the underlying principles are not hard to understand and an importer is well advised to be aware of them and the potential for cost saving which careful selection of the range of options available can provide. Goods need to be insured during transit against the following:

1. Perils in transit by sea, air, road or rail.
2. War risks, civil riot and 'commotion'.
3. Individual risks, such as pilferage or damage by seawater.

In addition, it is advisable for an importer to cover the *transaction itself* against political risks, non-performance by the supplier and the new law concerning product liability. The stages of transportation of the goods which need to be covered by insurance are as follows:

1. Transportation from exporter's premises to place of shipment.
2. Time delays which involve warehousing whilst awaiting shipment.
3. During transportation from point of exit to point of entry.
4. Offloading and storage in the United Kingdom awaiting collection.
5. Transportation to final destination.

The point at which responsibility for covering the risks is handed over to the importer depends on the terms of transportation agreed between him, his shipping agent and the exporter. In making such a choice, the importer should bear in mind that, in selecting CIF terms, the responsibility for insurance is left to the exporter. The policy he takes out may be with a local foreign insurance company and there may therefore be difficulties in understanding or interpreting the conditions laid down in them if anything goes wrong. In the United Kingdom, insurance transactions are governed by the Marine Insurance Act 1906, although, in practice, many of its provisions can be modified or circumvented by the insertion of special clauses in the policies. The Act lays down the essentials which must be included in all marine policies as follows:

1. The name of the assured or his agent.
2. The subject matter of the insurance.
3. The risks covered.
4. The journey and/or period of time the policy covers.
5. The sum insured.
6. The insurer's name.

If the route is laid down in the policy and is deviated from, then the insurance underwriters are released from liability, unless the deviation is due to the need to ensure the safety of the vessel, or to circumstances beyond the control of the shipping company or ship's master or to the necessity to give aid to ships in distress or to save life. A claim may also fail if the underwriters can establish that damage has been due to faulty packaging, so agreement on packaging to be used is a vital part of the terms and conditions of the order itself. If goods are sold whilst in transit, then the insurance cover can be reassigned to the purchaser by endorsement.

An importer may cover 'worldwide' for movements from anywhere to anywhere else by any approved method of transport. The common basis for valuing consignments for insurance is the CIF value plus 10 per cent, but any reasonable uplift or addition may be negotiated with the underwriter. A lower rate of premium applies to 'Duty insurance', where the risk does not commence until most marine perils no longer apply.

The two types of policy are:

1. *An 'open' policy* which, on payment of an adequate deposit, covers all shipments made up to a specific date for a specific amount.
2. *A 'floating' policy* which, on payment of a lump sum, covers each shipment as it is made, until the premium payment has been used up.

Premiums are normally collected monthly in arrears and are settled on a monthly scheduling basis. Although the Marine Insurance Act 1906 is designed primarily to cover transport by sea, its principles and protection apply equally to other forms of transport. Arrangements for insurance of road and rail freight therefore follow similar forms and can normally be made either directly with the freight carrier, an insurance broker or a freight forwarder.

The exception is the case of airfreight insurance, where airlines normally accept responsibility if an aircraft is lost or damaged up to a certain value per kilo (the equivalent of the FPA terms of a marine policy). Additional cover therefore needs to be arranged if the cargo is of a higher value or the other risks need to be covered and this can be arranged either with the airline directly or with a forwarding agent. Once arrangements have been made and terms agreed for the initial shipment, they can usually be allowed to stand for all future shipments of the same type of goods from the same source.

In the case of insurance of the transaction itself, there are two main classes of risk to cover:

1. Those arising from non-performance by the supplier.
2. Those arising under the new law of product liability.

To cover either of these classes of risk, it is necessary to use an insurance broker.

Non-performance by the supplier may arise from situations both inside and outside his control, but in any case the results from the importer's point of view are the same, particularly if, in his turn, he has contractual obligations to his own customers. The main risks in this area are as follows:

1. The operational failure of the supplier to meet his delivery dates.
2. Sudden insolvency of the supplier.
3. The confiscation or nationalisation of the supplier's business.
4. The inability of the supplier to ship goods as a result of political embargoes.
5. The refusal of a state trading nation's selling organisation to honour obligations it has undertaken, chiefly as a result of its government's control of foreign exchange levels.
6. Either the cancellation or sudden imposition of import quotas by the UK government, particularly on textile and clothing under the MFA regime, as a result of a sudden surge in import penetration in the products concerned (*see* section 4.2.5).

It is now possible, through a specialist insurance underwriter, to cover up to 95 per cent of these risks with a 'supplier default' and/or a 'political risks' policy. Clearly it is necessary for an importer to balance the additional cost of such cover against the probability of their happening and the possible losses he might incur if they do.

Product liability insurance is another animal altogether. The concept of 'no-fault' liability was first developed in the United States during the 1960s through successive rulings of the Supreme Court. There it has led to crippling damages being awarded to litigants against manufacturers fundamentally because, the US law allows an attorney to base his fees solely on a large percentage of any damages he can obtain and juries to decide on the level of damages to be awarded, neither of which is permitted under UK law.

Currently, in the United Kingdom, as in most other European countries, the law of product liability requires that a plaintiff who has received injury as a result of using a product has to prove negligence or faulty workmanship on the part of the manufacturer before he can receive compensation. In particular, unless an importer has a specific contract with *his* customer, then he stands a good chance of avoiding product liability, even if the product is faulty and has caused the injury. The underlying problem is that in any action involving product liability, the good reputation of the producer or retailer is at stake. Therefore he feels compelled to defend even the most trivial charges against him, frequently on purely technical or legal grounds. There is little scope for generosity of treatment in such a situation.

'No-fault' liability however means just that. Under such a regime, the user can obtain compensation from the producer simply because he produced it, without any requirement to prove or imply negligence on the producer's part. The report of the UK Law Commission on the subject, stated the underlying principle involved as being that 'loss should lie with the party best able to exercise safety and quality control over the product who can cover the risk by insurance'. There is no necessary implication of guilt or fault implied. If such conditions do amount to criminal negligence, then there is the possibility of criminal action against the producer as well as the civil action for damages.

Since the 1970s, first the Council of Europe and later the EEC have interested themselves in this concept. In 1977, the Council of Europe produced the Strasbourg Convention which provided for the strict liability of producers for products which caused 'personal injury or death' and each signatory of the Convention (which included the United Kingdom) agreed to introduce national laws which conformed to it. In parallel, the EEC Commission had begun work on the drafting of a Council Directive on the same subject, which differed in a number of respects from the Strasbourg Convention. The most significant difference was that it did not confine liability to personal injury or death but extended it to damage to private property. The argument of producers against the proposal was that such a liability would inhibit technological innovation and development, because it would be difficult and expensive to insure against the eventuality. The main controversy therefore has been whether or not to include as a possible defence what is known as the 'state of the art'. Such a defence would allow producers to argue that, at the time of the product's development, there was no means of knowing scientifically that the injury might be caused.

On 25 July 1985 the EEC Council of Ministers adopted Directive 85/374/EEC which set out the guidelines for member state legislation which was to be introduced by 20 July 1988. The Directive places responsibility for a product firmly on the producer of the finished product, of components or of natural products contained in it. The term 'producer' is extended to include those who present a product under their own brand name, traders who refuse to disclose their source of supply and, most significant of all, importers. It permits member states to limit liability in any one case to £50 million and to introduce a 'state of the art' clause in their national legislation if they so wish. It does, however, deny compensation to the user of an inherently risky product (say a cigarette) if it can be established that the user knew the risks he was undertaking when he used or consumed the product. The Directive limits liability to only one European importer. Thus, if a UK importer buys imported goods from a French importer, then only the French importer can be proceeded against but if it is the other way round, then the UK importer is liable.

The UK Consumer Protection Act 1987, which incorporates the provisions of the Directive into UK law, places no limit on compensation but does specifically exclude primary agricultural products. It also allows seven possible defences, namely:

1. that the defect was not in the product supplied;
2. that the product was a safe component and the defect was in the final product;
3. that the defect was beyond present scientific knowledge;
4. that means to discover the defect were not available;
5. that the defect was caused by compliance with the law;
6. that the producer did not supply the goods;
7. that the supplier was not a trader.

Here again, with this new legislation pending, the importer needs to consult his insurance broker, asking for quotations for product liability cover and, in particular, what are the terms and conditions on offer.

A second precaution for an importer to take, especially with new products, is to submit the product to an authorised testing house to ensure that it meets British Standards Institution standards (*see* section 5.2.5). Even if the product does pass this test, it does not provide a defence against a 'no-fault' liability claim but it does at least indicate to the importer any likely dangers inherent in the product. Such certificates might help in negotiating insurance terms and cover.

A third precaution is for an importer to include in the terms and conditions of purchase a complete indemnity clause from the supplier in the importer's favour. However, if a serious injury does occur, there could well be difficulties in persuading the supplier to honour it. In such circumstances, some kind of bond guarantee might be sought, although it all adds to the cost of the product. Certainly, if an indemnity clause can be negotiated, then the importer should ask his supplier to nominate a UK agent on whom any process can be served.

A fourth precaution, if an importer is selling components for incorporation into his customer's products, is, if possible, to obtain an indemnity from the customer. A final precaution is for the importer to maintain strict records of where goods come from and to whom they are sold. The object is to provide a legal 'audit trail' if it becomes necessary to consider passing off a claim. Such records would need to be maintained for the ten years which is the limitation period laid down in the legislation.

6.3.3 Taking delivery of goods from the carrier

Before goods are presented for customs clearance, they must first be handed over by the carrier to the importer or his agent according to set procedures. Before the carrier will release the goods, the importer or his agent must produce an original copy of the bill of lading or its equivalent used for other methods of transport and pay the necessary dock wharfage and port dues. These payments are usually settled by regular users either on a monthly account basis or through a deposit scheme. If freight and shipping charges have already been paid by the overseas supplier or the importer's agent, then the bill of lading will be endorsed 'To bearer'. If not, then the importer will also have to make arrangements to pay these charges before the goods are released to him.

If the goods arrive before the bill of lading, then the importer can obtain release of the goods by taking out a 'letter of indemnity' and presenting the bill of lading to the carrier when it does arrive. The letter of indemnity must indicate the distinguishing marks and contents of consignments and the name of the carrying vessel. It may be necessary for the importer to arrange for his bank to guarantee this letter.

If the goods are not for immediate use, they can be sent to a warehouse approved by Customs and the payment of duty can be deferred until they are brought into free circulation in the United Kingdom. It is also necessary to check that all documents which are needed to support the bill of lading are available and in order before the consignment arrives at the place of entry. These documents vary according to the type of goods and the country of origin.

With airfreight, the air waybill effectively replaces the bill of lading for most purposes of customs procedures. In the case of arrival by road or rail, the appropriate Community transit document or TIR carnet replaces the bill of lading. Once the goods have been collected from the carrier, they must be presented for customs clearance before they leave the boundaries of the place of entry.

6.4 ENTRY PROCEDURES AND DOCUMENTATION

6.4.1 Customs procedures in general

Since Britian joined the European Community in 1972, HM Customs and Excise collects Customs duty and other imposts on behalf of the Community, retaining only an agreed percentage as an administration charge. The procedures, therefore, for customs clearance are those laid down by the EEC Customs Union, which is a branch of the Commission itself. Customs Notice 483 provides a concise introduction to customs entry procedures and more detailed information about documentation is contained in *The Integrated Tariff of the United Kingdom* Volume 3, which includes reference to changes made in Customs 88 (*see* section 6.2).

Once goods have been taken over from the carrier, either by the importer or his agent, they must be presented for customs clearance. For this purpose the Customs Office will require the appropriate entry form and supporting documents, which will vary according to the type and status of the goods. Details of these requirements are set out in Customs Notice 484 (July 1987), sections 1.4.2, 3.1 and 3.8. Since 1 January 1988, the standard import entry form has been the C88 (the single administrative document). Which type of C88 is to be used depends on the type and source of the product, whether the entry is to be processed manually or by computer and whether or not it forms part of a consolidated consignment (*see* section 3.5.2).

The computer system at present in use by HM Customs is the Departmental Entry Processing System (DEPS). This maintains a central record of entry transactions based on information reported on the import entry form. Terminals located at certain points of entry and other locations can input information into it and interrogate it directly through a modem network based on the telephone system. There are two basic systems with access to the DEPS computer:

1. The customs import entry system (CIE).
2. The direct trader input system (DTI).

Under the *customs import entry* system, the terminals are installed in customs offices and operated by customs staff on the basis of information lodged with them by importers and their agents. This system operates at the following points of entry: Dover (East and West Docks), Folkestone, Liverpool Docks, London Docks, Tilbury Docks. Input is based on information provided on the single administrative document (SAD) and the procedures are set out in detail in Customs Notice 484, section 1.4.2.

Under the *direct trader input* system, importers or their agents are given direct access to DEPS through their own terminals. This system operates at the following entry points:

Bellport
Chatham
Felixstowe
Gatwick Airport
Great Yarmouth
Grimsby
Harwich
Heathrow Airport
Hull
Immingham
Ipswich
Manchester Airport
Manchester Docks
Poole
Portsmouth
Ramsgate
Rochester
Sheerness
Southampton
Sutton Freight Terminal
Teesport

Again, details of the procedures to be used under DTI are set out in Customs Notice 484, section 1.4.2. Goods entering in any sealed container/vehicle do not necessarily have to clear Customs at the point of entry (*see* section 6.3.1).

Under these two computer systems (CIE and DTI), the computer prints out an endorsed customs removal note (C130) clearing the goods and authorising collection. At the time of writing, all other points of entry continue to operate manual systems, which are described in the same section of Customs Notice 484.

Under the *local import control* system, importers who handle at least ten full container loads a month can arrange for the containers to pass through Customs under seal and to be cleared by customs officials at the point of unloading which can be their own premises. Details of this procedure are set out in Customs Notice 464A.

Furthermore, the *period entry* system allows organisations who engage in large-scale, repetitive import transactions using their own computers to notify the initial arrival of the goods on a simplified form of the C88 which requires only the most basic information needed to identify the shipment at the point of entry. The importer's computer then picks up the remaining entry details from its records and consolidates them on to a periodic import schedule. This is sent monthly to Customs, who produce a summary of the duty and VAT which has been deferred during the month and the importer settles 15 days later. Details of this procedure are set out in Customs Notice 480 and in Notice 484, section 3.3.

Most goods which enter the country do so free of customs duty if they are coming from sources within the European Community's trading regime or are entitled to other forms of preferential treatment. However, although Community goods may have conformed to import formalities and paid EEC Customs charges at their original point of entry, they could still be liable for

ENTRY PROCEDURES AND DOCUMENTATION 117

1. CAP monetary compensation amounts (*see* section 4.3.4).
2. Anti-dumping duties.
3. National taxes such as VAT.

Special provisions are also in force for the new member states which are still in a state of transition towards full membership, i.e. Greece, Spain and Portugal. Details of these procedures are set out in Customs Notice 750B.

Apart from differences in the movement procedures between ship, road, rail and air described in section 6.3.1, there are also certain differences between the procedures for intra-Community trade and trade with the rest of the world.

The *Community transit* system (CT) is designed to exploit the advantages of the European Community's Customs Union for its member states. The elements of the system are:

1. The introduction of identification measures at the point of exportation for goods which hold 'Community status' and which may therefore enter other member states free of duty.
2. The facility to move goods easily within the Community whilst protecting the national taxes which member states are permitted to collect on them.

'Community status' is defined as applying to goods which have conformed to EEC Regulation 227/77, that is to say, they have satisfied the conditions of articles 9 and 10 of the Treaty of Rome by having originated in the EEC, or having originated in a third country but are in free circulation within the Community by virtue of having complied with import facilities and been levied with the appropriate EEC duties and other charges due on them.

The full CT procedure works as follows:

1. The trader who undertakes responsibility for transporting goods from one member state to another raises and distributes the appropriate copies of the C88 form and its supporting documents.
2. He is required to provide a guarantee or cash deposit to cover any additional EEC charges or national dues which might arise. The precise form of such guarantees is laid down in Appendices F, G and H of Customs Notice 750.
3. The importer or his agent must clear the goods by presenting them, together with the appropriate copy of the C88 and supporting documents, to the Customs authority in the importing member state. Once a C88 has been raised under CT procedures, it *must* be presented, whether or not Community status is subsequently being claimed.
4. Customs at the point of arrival duly notifies the clearance of the goods to

the customs authorities at the point of departure and the exporting trader is released from his guarantee.

Full details of the system are set out in Customs Notices 750 and 484, section 3.6. To speed up entry further, arrangements can be made to defer the payment of VAT under special deposit or guarantee scheme (*see* section 7.2.2).

There are special arrangements for goods which are intended for re-exportation and application for these should be made in good time. In the case of textiles and clothing, Form Ex/A or B should be sent to the **Department of Trade and Industry**, **CTP Division**, Sunley Tower, Piccadilly Plaza, Manchester M1 4BA. In the case of non-textiles, Form ILB/REx should be sent to the **Department of Trade and Industry**, 2–18 Ebury Bridge Road, London SW1W 8QD. If goods are to be processed before re-exportation, then additional documentation is required under inward/outward processing rules (*see* section 6.4.6). Payment of duty on goods which are not immediately required for use may be postponed by storing them in customs warehouses approved by the Customs and Excise. Full details of this procedure are provided in Customs Notice 232.

The additional procedures which apply to the various regimes, treaties, arrangements and preference schemes are described in sections 6.4.2–6.4.7 below.

6.4.2 State trading nations procedures

The STN regime, together with a listing of the countries involved in it, is described in section 3.1.1. Details of import procedures and the quotas which will be applied are published annually in one of the January issues of the DTI's weekly publication *British Business* under 'Notices to Importers'. Except in the case of the People's Republic of China, importers must obtain quota certificates from the appropriate state trading authority in the exporting country and present it, together with Form ILB/W, to the **Import Licensing Branch**, **Department of Trade and Industry**, 2–18 Ebury Bridge Road, London SW1W 8QD, who will then proceed to issue an import licence. Import licences are valid until 31 March of the year following their issue, always providing that the goods have been shipped before 31 December of the year of issue.

In the case of goods which fall within Common Agricultural Policy classifications, special forms of licences are required for most products and in many cases the products are also subject to health requirements (*see* section 4.3.4). Full details can be obtained from the **Intervention Board for Agricultural Products**, Fountain House, 2 Queen's Walk, Butts Centre, Reading RG1 7QW.

Certain clothing and textile products covered by the Multi Fibre Arrangement, even if not subject to quota, may be subject to surveillance licensing (*see* section 4.2.5) and details are set out in *British Business*, 26 Sept 1986, Notice to Importers No. 2096.

Imports from the People's Republic of China are import administered and import licences will be granted on the basis of past trade. Applications for import licences should be made before 30 January of the year concerned on Form ILB/W and the application should be supported by a statement of trade done in the products concerned over the previous three years. A pro forma for making this statement is available from the Import Licensing Board. The product categories which are an exception to this 'import administered' rule are domestic china and earthenware and restricted TV sets which are export controlled. For these products, the procedures are the same as those described above for other STNs.

6.4.3 The EEC preference schemes procedures

The European Community offers preferential trade treatment to the following:

1. The European Free Trade Association.
2. Its Mediterranean Associates.
3. The Lomé Convention countries.
4. Countries covered by the generalised scheme of preferences.

These schemes cover both ordinary merchandise and products covered by the Common Agricultural Policy. The classes of goods which are granted such preferences are set out in *The Tariff* (*see* section 6.1.3).

When imported goods are eligible under more than one of these schemes then the lowest entitlement rate applies. If the preferences are subject to quota or other forms of ceiling control, then, when the quotas are exhausted, normal duty can be reimposed and this may occur arbitrarily at any time during the trading year. Details of quotas and other controls are set out in Customs Notice 771. The conditions for admission of goods under a preference scheme are:

1. that they must be describable in terms of the qualifying tariff heading;
2. that they can be established as originating in a preferential country; and
3. that they must normally have been conveyed directly from the country of origin to the European Community without being split *en route* (although there are transit procedures available for landlocked originating countries – see Customs Notice 826).

Rules of origin vary according to the particular preference scheme. The general rule is that they must have been 'wholly produced' in the preferential source country. However, for some schemes relating to developing countries, the goods can be partially produced in a number of countries within the group and the final product deemed to be 'wholly produced'. This is known as the 'cumulation rule'.

The exporter must produce adequate documentary evidence of origin, normally in the form of a 'movement certificate'. However, in the case of the generalised scheme of preferences (GSP), a 'Form A' certificate of origin, issued and stamped by the governmental authority in the exporting country, is necessary. A telecopy facsimile of either the movement certificate or Form A is acceptable for clearance purposes, providing that the original is produced within 14 days of the arrival of the goods.

If goods consigned to the United Kingdom enter the Community through another member state, then the UK importer must obtain a 'replacement certificate' from the EEC consignor, duly certified by the Customs authority in the consignor's country. A movement certificate or Form A are normally valid for a specific period of some four to five months.

6.4.4 The Multi Fibre Arrangement procedures

The annual quota for each category of the Multi Fibre Arrangement is published in the *Official Journal of the European Community* and in *British Business*, Notices to Importers, in the first January issue.

For goods imported under this regime, importers must obtain an export certificate from their overseas supplier and forward it, together with Form ILB/W, to the **Import Licensing Branch, Department of Trade and Industry**, 2–18 Ebury Bridge Road, London SW1W 8QD, who will then issue the appropriate import licence. Such licences are valid until 31 March of the following year providing the goods have been shipped before the end of the year of issue.

In quotas for 1987 onwards, imports of a certain proportion of children's garments will be licensed in the ratio of five child to three adult garments. In these cases, the licensing authorities in the exporting countries will endorse the export licence with the phrase 'for garments of a commercial size not exceeding 130 centimetres'. The import licence issued by the DTI will specify that the goods are for use by children of body height not exceeding 130 centimetres.

Importers should exercise particular care when buying MFA goods which have already been imported into other member states, because they are not automatically deemed to be in free Community circulation. If the United Kingdom's quota has already been filled, then the UK may have invoked Article 115 of the Treaty of Rome to prevent the quota-sharing arrangement being circumvented. If Article 115 has been applied, then bad luck. The European Court of Justice has already upheld the use of Article 115 as a means of preventing this particular circumvention. Perhaps an importer's best safeguard is to use 'Delivered Duty Paid' rather than, say, CIF, as the terms of such a deal. Then, if the supplier cannot pass the goods through UK Customs, the importer does not have to pay for them.

Apart from the dual licensing documentation, the procedures and documentation for imports under the MFA are as described in section 6.4.1.

6.4.5 Common Agricultural Policy procedures

The principles underlying the European Community's Common Agricultural Policy are described in section 4.3.4, and the import procedures and documentation relating to it in Customs Notices 780, 781, 782 and 790.

To say that the procedures are inclined to be complicated is the understatement of the century. However, when despair approaches, help and advice can be obtained from the **Intervention Board for Agricultural Products (IBAP)** at POB 69, Fountain House, 2 Queen's Walk, Reading RG1 7QW (telephone: 0734 58368).

As with customs duty, agricultural levies imposed under the CAP are collected by HM Customs and Excise on behalf of the European Community. Clearance procedures therefore are laid down by Community regulations, which are published in its *Official Journal* and circulated in the United Kingdom in the form of Customs Notices. Customs Notice 790 provides general information about the CAP, including, in Appendix A, a badly-needed glossary of terms and abbreviations. The goods covered by the CAP are listed in Amendment Slip No. 1 to the Notice's Appendix B. Customs Notice 780 describes the specific CAP import procedures. These procedures cover two basic situations: CAP goods imported from other member states, and CAP goods imported from non-member states.

CAP goods imported from member states are subject only to adjustment payments known as monetary compensation amounts (MCAs). These adjustments are necessary because European farmers are entitled to receive the appropriate 'market support price' for any CAP goods they produce. If the open market price falls below the support price, then the European Commission intervenes to buy the goods at the support price, puts them into circulation at that price and stores any surpluses which the market cannot absorb. This support price is set annually in terms of the European currency unit (ECU) and, for CAP support purposes, is converted into the national currencies of member states at special 'green' rates which are fixed at the same time.

During the course of the year, the 'green' rates frequently differ from the current market exchange rate. So, to ensure that trade in CAP products is not distorted by transactions designed purely to take advantage of this fact, CAP trade between member states is subject to price adjustments designed to compensate for these fluctuations. It is these adjustments which are called MCAs. The current MCA rates can always be obtained from any Customs and Excise entry processing unit (EPU) which are located at all points of entry.

When CAP goods are traded between member states, their customs authorities pay to, and collect from the exporter both the export and import MCA dues under what is known as the 'exporter pays' system. This avoids double accounting within the Community.

CAP goods imported from non-member states may be subject to Customs duty, agricultural levies, monetary compensation amounts (MCAs), and Licensing requirements. *Customs duty* is the normal impost levied under the Tariff. *Agricultural levies* are countervailing charges which are designed to bring the imported price of CAP goods to the level of the Community's 'market support price'. These levies are applied before duty is calculated. *MCAs* are applied to the final price to bring the 'market support price' to terms with the national currency of the importing member state. *Licensing requirements* are also placed on certain CAP goods, partly to provide statistics on sensitive goods, and partly to enable the Community to manage the market. It does this by altering the level of levies and refunds or, in the last resort, by restricting trade altogether. Such licences are issued by the IBAP (*see* above), which also issues details of which goods are subject to licensing requirements in a series of 'EM leaflets' which can be obtained from the same address.

So far, the CAP procedural system has been relatively straightforward. Now for the difficult part. Imposts on CAP goods from non-member states take a number of different forms, namely,

1. Levies, which are straightforward charges, normally in addition to any Community Tariff dues.
2. Countervailing duties, which are applied normally on a seasonal basis only.
3. Variable charges, which are applied to products processed from certain basic CAP products and are designed to protect the Community processors rather than the farmer.
4. Additional duties, which are sometimes applied to sugar and flour for further arcane reasons.

The special requirements relating to Customs entry procedure and documentation for CAP goods are set out in Customs Notice 484, section 3.7.1. The importer is responsible for calculating all levies and MCAs and entering them on the appropriate entry form according to the formulae laid down in Section III and Appendix B of CN 780.

6.4.6 Outward and inward processing relief

The principles governing outward and inward processing relief have already been discussed in section 3.4.2. In the United Kingdom, relief procedures are laid down under the Import Duty (Outward Processing Relief) Regulations of 1976 and the Agricultural Levies (Outward Processing Relief) Order of 1976. The conditions for obtaining such relief are as follows:

1. Customs and Excise must be informed before the materials or components are first exported.
2. The value of the exported goods must be clearly established.
3. On re-entry, Customs and Excise must be able to satisfy themselves that the declared quantities of the right materials are included in the finished product. This is normally established by defining the 'rate of yield' on the original application form. The rate of yield is a calculation of the quantity of manufactured goods which can be made from a specific quantity of the goods exported (e.g. how many handkerchiefs from a kilogram of cotton fabric).

If the process of assembling or manufacturing the materials or components into a finished product changes is tarriff classification (as it normally would), then the country of origin changes to that of the manufacturer (*see* section 6.4.8).

For OPR, the following relevant forms can be obtained from Customs and Excise:

1. C&E 1152   Authorisation of OP relief and confirmation of shipment.
2. C&E 1173   Shipping or postal bill.
3. C&E 1154   Claim for OPR on re-entry.
4. C105   Declaration of *ad valorem* import value (where applicable).
5. C179   Claim for relief from VAT (where applicable).
6. C&E 1155   Information sheet when triangulation procedure is adopted.

Fuller details of the OPR process, including a description of the method of assessing duty payable on the value added during processing, are contained in Customs Notice No. 235 May 1978.

There are two methods of claiming IPR:

1. *Suspension*, whereby the manufacturer does not have to pay duty on entry. This method is used when the manufacturer clearly intends to export his total production of the goods manufactured from the imported materials or components.
2. *Drawback*, whereby the manufacturer pays duty on the imports, but claims it back when the finished goods are re-exported. This method is used when the manufacturer is uncertain about how much of his production of the goods concerned will be re-exported and how much sold on the domestic market.

Relief is claimed:

1. Under a *General Authority*, which covers all goods not listed in Appendix A of Customs Notice 221 and can be invoked by quoting the relevant General Authority number on the Customs entry form.
2. Under a *Special Authority*, which is required for all goods listed in Appendix A of Customs Notice No. 221. Application in these cases must be made on C&E Form 810 before importation takes place.

For IPR, the relevant documents are:

1. C&E 810   IPR application form.
2. C&E 811   Transfer of IPR goods.
3. C&E 812   Suspension return.
4. C&E 813   Drawback return.
5. C88   IPR export form.

Fuller details of the IPR process are contained in Customs Notice No. 221, December 1986.

6.4.7 Free trade zones procedures

The potential advantages to importers in free trade zones have already been discussed in section 3.5.3. The procedures for using free zone facilities are relatively simple and can be summarised as follows:

1. Within 14 days of shipping goods into a zone, the importer or his agent must complete and lodge with the freeport authority the three-part 'free zone status document' (STATDOC) which is, in effect an application for freeport status for the goods.
2. The freeport authority converts this information into a computerised 'freeport input document' (FID) and allocates to the consignment an individual FZL number.
3. The goods can then be released by the freeport authority either for warehousing within the free zone (by issue of a 'freeport release for

warehousing' (FRW) or to the care of the importer's agent (by the issue of a 'freeport release authority' (FRA)).

This is all that is necessary so long as the goods remain within the free zone without changing ownership or being consumed. What happens next depends on the nature of the transaction. If it is decided to move the goods into the hinterland:

1. The importer or his agent must initiate normal customs entry procedures, and arrange to pay the necessary duty, levies and VAT to the customs authorities. In exchange he will receive from them an 'out of charge note' (C 130).
2. On production of this note, the freeport authorities will issue a 'freight exit document' (FED), which authorises the importer or his agent to move the goods out of the free zone.

If the importer decides to re-export the goods directly to a foreign destination, then he is required to follow the normal export procedures and documentation set out in Customs Notice 484 (July 1987).

Any importer who wishes to explore the possibility of using free zone facilities should contact his nearest freeport authority who will provide him with all the advice and information he needs for his particular operation.

6.4.8 Rules of origin

The origin of imported goods is important because it determines whether or not they qualify for any of the various preferential treatments available under the network of international trade agreements to which the United Kingdom is party. Unfortunately, the rules of origin vary slightly but significantly from agreement to agreement but the general rules which determine origin are as follows:

1. They must have been produced wholly in the country concerned.
2. The materials or components have been subject to 'sufficient transformation' in the country concerned to change their nature.

For most practical purposes, 'sufficient transformation' is deemed to have taken place if, in the course of processing or assembling a product it changes its tariff classification, i.e. Tariff coding and thus, for Customs purposes, becomes to all intents and purposes a different product.

For the purposes of defining origin, the member states of the European Community are treated as one and so too are the members of EFTA. The rules of origin for the different trade regimes are set out in Customs Notice 828 *EEC Preferences – Rules of Origin* and its subsequent amendments.

Most agreements which grant preferences require that the documents relating to the importation of the goods include an official Certificate of Origin which is provided either by the government or the local chamber of commerce of the exporting country. Clothing and textiles which are subject to MFA quotas and have already entered the Community through another member state and been charged to its quota share and are then re-exported to the United Kingdom under the rules of free circulation, also need a certificate of origin. This enables the necessary adjustment to be made to the member state quota records. Since the repeal of the relevent sections of the Trade Descriptions Act 1968, it is no longer necessary to label imported goods with their country of origin.

6.4.9 Customs valuation

The rules for valuing goods for Customs purposes can become very complicated and are explained in detail in Customs Notice 252 *Valuation of Imported Goods for Customs Purposes, VAT and Trade Statistics* and in *The Integrated Tariff of the United Kingdom,* Volume I, section 14 (*see* section 6.2.3). The rules for deriving Customs valuation are based on the GATT Valuation Code and are set out in various EEC Regulations which are fully listed in CN252. As the Notice states, HM Customs requires that imported goods be valued for three purposes:

1. To assess the duty payable.
2. To assess VAT.
3. To enable collection and publication of UK and EEC trade statistics.

In practice, this means that each consignment can have three different values. Attempts to reconcile the three sets of statistics which emerge from them is not to be recommended as a participant sport.

For the purpose of assessing duty payable, Customs use one of two methods of valuation:

1. By 'measured unit' regardless of value of contents.
2. By value of goods (*ad valorem*).

The *'unit measurement'* is usually adopted for levying on 'excise' items such as wines, spirits and tobacco where the intrinsic value of the contents can be comparatively low.

'Ad valorem' is the most commonly-adopted method of valuing goods for Customs purposes and there are six methods of calculation as follows:

1. The 'transaction method', which is based on the price paid by the importer to his overseas supplier as evidenced in the invoice or its

equivalent. The 'equivalent' includes telex or similar messages. For the purpose of valuation by this method, it is advisable to lay down in the terms and conditions of the order or contract a very specific layout for the invoice, because the rules of valuation for Customs purposes under it, as defined in CN252, set out in detail what is to be both included and excluded in the price for purposes of valuation. Inclusions comprise, besides actual manufacturing costs:

a. delivery costs;
b. commissions and brokerage;
c. royalties and licence fees which are a condition of sale;
d. goods or services provided by the seller free or at reduced cost;
e. containers and packaging;
f. any proceeds of resale shared with the seller.

Exclusions comprise:
a. delivery costs within the European Community;
b. Community duties and taxes already paid;
c. taxes paid in country of origin;
d. discounts;
e. cost of related marketing activities including advertising, promotion, warranty or guarantee services;
f. commission paid by the importer to agents representing him outside the European Community;
g. certain interest charges;
h. rights of reproduction;
i. post-importation work on imported industrial plant and machinery;
j. cost incurred by supplier in procuring quota or other forms of export licences.

In all exclusion cases, the importer must be prepared to support his claim with adequate documentary evidence.

There are, in addition, specific rules about valuations if intermediaries such as commission agents or branch offices are utilised by the vendor in the United Kingdom. These are detailed in Appendices E and F of CN252.

When using customs input entry (CIE) procedures described in section 6.4.1, calculations must be shown on a Value Build-up Sheet (Form C89).

If, for one reason or another, it is not possible to determine the 'transaction value' in these specific terms, then one of the other five methods may be used.

2. Based on customs value of identical goods imported into the Community.

3. Based on the customs value of similar good imported into the Community.
4. Based on the selling price of the goods in the EEC.
5. Based on the production cost of the goods in the EEC.
6. Based on any other reasonable means of calculating valuation based on GATT rules.

These situations (2–6) normally occur for example in transactions between the various national subsidiaries of multinational companies.

There are also simplified procedures for valuing perishable items (notably fresh fruit and vegetables) and special arrangements for computer software, 'free of charge' goods and used goods, all of which are set out in CN252.

A further complication can arise in valuation for customs purposes if all or part of the invoices for goods or services are expressed in foreign currency. These must be converted into sterling at the prevailing customs exchange rate, unless the contract lays down specifically that settlement must be made in sterling at an agreed fixed rate. Customs exchange rates are fixed weekly, are posted in local VAT offices and at entry points and are available on Prestel (page 500085). Rates for currencies other than those shown on these lists can be obtained from the **Customs Valuation Branch**, telephone 01-382 5955 and 5960.

If it is not possible, for any reason, to arrive at the Customs value by any of the methods listed above, then goods can still be released against a 'GO12/30' deposit and the value can be adjusted later when it is established. The Customs and Excise Management Act 1979, in section 127, also provides for independent arbitration if an importer disagrees with the Customs valuation.

It is the responsibility of the importer to establish, and if necessary justify, the initial valuation of the goods he imports. An importer exercises this responsibility for consignments of over £1,300 in value by completing a valuation declaration form, either C105A or B and presenting it to the Customs Office with the other clearance documents at point of entry.

Alternatively, if an importer is importing regularly the same type of goods (in Tariff code terms) from one or more suppliers, he may take out a 'season ticket' in the form of a 'general valuation statement' by completing either C109A (for method 1 valuations) or C109B (for methods 2–6). Such statements are normally valid for three years. It will be necessary for the importer to send a copy of the C109 to each agent that he decides to employ.

The same procedure applies to the Period Entry System (*see* section 6.4.1).

Valuation for statistical purposes is dealt with in section 6.4.11.

6.4.10 Suspension of duty

Customs duty can be suspended altogether on the following types of goods:

1. Instruments imported for scientific research.
2. Goods for industrial research.
3. Goods for the handicapped.

Further information about these reliefs can be obtained from the **Department of Trade and Industry**, CRE/4D, Sanctuary Buildings, 16–20 Great Smith Street, London SW1P 3DB. (telephone: 01-215 5968).

It is also possible to obtain temporary suspension of duty on certain classes of raw material and components which are not being produced in the European Community. This dispensation is designed to ensure that the UK manufacturing industries which are partly or wholly dependent on raw materials which are not available from within the Community are not disadvantaged in terms of international competitiveness by this fact. Further information about this type of relief is available from the **Department of Trade and Industry, ITP Division**, Room 437, 1 Victoria Street, London SW1H 0ET (telephone: 01-215 3576).

6.4.11 Trade statistics

HM Customs has been responsible for the collection of trade statistics for the Department of Trade in one form or another since 1696. Today, without such information, it would be virtually impossible to conduct the negotiation of international trade treaties and agreements. The information (together with the inferences drawn from it, often in a highly selective way) provides the bulk of the ammunition used in the running battle between the protectionist and free trade factions.

A typical example of how trade statistics are brought selectively into play by pressure groups occurred some years ago under the Multi-Fibre Arrangement. One of the grounds for introducing new quotas under the 'basket extractor mechanism' (*see* section 4.2.5) is 'severe market disruption in the importing country'. This is commonly measured in terms of 'market penetration'. Market penetration is calculated by expressing imports as a percentage of domestic consumption of the category of goods under threat. The higher the percentage, the higher the market penetration. High and growing import penetration is deemed to be clear and sufficient evidence of pending market disruption. This duly occurred in the case of ladies' dresses and so the manufacturers' lobby immediately demanded the imposition of quotas. Unfortunately, one problem with this internationally-recognised method of measuring market penetration is that it takes no account whatsoever of export performance. In the case of ladies' dresses, it so happened that at the time imports were growing, the United Kingdom was an overall net exporter and exports were also growing! Such aberrations notwithstanding, trade statistics are still the most effective way of monitoring the orderly conduct of international trade.

Customs collect the necessary data for these statistics from the Customs entry forms. The subsequent method of valuing the goods for statistical purposes is outlined in Part III of Customs Notice 252. It differs from the other valuations of goods because of the necessity to express the figures in terms of equivalent CIF values, which is the common international standard used for the measurement of import trade flows. HM Customs data is also utilised by the European Commission Customs Union and OECD in compiling their international statistics.

In the United Kingdom, trade statistics are published monthly in *Overseas Trade Statistics*, copies of which are available from HM Stationery Office. In addition, Customs make available through marketing agents more detailed information analysed in terms of country of origin, country of consignment, country of destination, point of entry or shipment and by nationality and type of transportation used. These disaggregations are taken down to the level of the nine-figure TARIC Code (*see* section 6.2.3). The DTI publishes quarterly summaries of these trade statistics in their weekly publication *British Business*.

7

IMPORT FINANCE

7.1 PAYMENTS TO BE MADE

7.1.1 Customs duty and excise

HM Customs and Excise are responsible for collecting all duty and excise charges at the point of entry unless other arrangements have been agreed. For all practical purposes, duty and excise on imported goods are treated as one. In effect, excise charged on imports is a countervailing duty designed to bring imported goods to competitive terms with similar domestically-produced goods. Excise charges on domestically-produced goods are subject to a different collection regime.

Importers can make arrangements with Customs and Excise to defer the payment of import duties in the following circumstances:

1. By negotiating a 15–45-day deferment covered by a guarantee (usually provided by a bank) that payment will be forthcoming on the due date.
2. By storing goods in a Customs-approved general or franchise warehouse until they are cleared or needed.
3. By holding goods in a freeport until they are needed.
4. By taking advantage of the customs period entry or direct trader input schemes to clear goods on periodic import schedules rather than on individual entry forms (*see* section 6.4.1).

7.1.2 Value added tax

HM Customs and Excise are also responsible for collecting VAT at the time and place of entry unless other arrangements have been made. Such payments by importers can of course be treated as inputs in the usual way and claimed back on their periodic VAT returns. Again, by providing a suitable guarantee of eventual payment, an importer can make arrangements to defer and consolidate VAT payments for up to 45 days.

In order to provide evidence that VAT has been settled, each importer or agent must have been allocated a 'Trader Unique Reference Number' (TURN), which comprises his VAT registration number plus a three-digit suffix. Importers who are not registered in this way should apply on Form C1416, which can be obtained from any local Customs or VAT office. Details of this scheme are set out in Customs Notice 101 (April 1986).

7.2 METHODS OF FINANCING IMPORTS

7.2.1 Loans, guarantees and discounts

The main proposition on which banks and finance houses have grown fat over the centuries is that exporters want to be paid as fast as possible and importers want to pay as late as possible. The gap between these two aspirations can be filled in a number of ways, all of which involve costs which must be passed to the final consumer. The cost of such bridging facilities depends on two factors:

1. The current going price for money in the international financial markets.
2. The risk that the transaction will, for one reason or another, not be completed. Banks rarely provide bridging facilities of this sort without being provided with some form of collateral *and* adequate insurance of the risk involved. (This being so, the gap between the rates at which they borrow their money and those they charge to their borrowers is at times hard to understand or justify.)

It is also possible for the overseas exporter to obtain accommodation from any export support scheme which his government offers. Importers should seek to discuss such facilities with their suppliers, but may well find them uncommunicative if such discussions are associated too closely with price negotiations! If an importer decides to maintain his liquidity by borrowing to support his import transactions, then the following range of facilities is available:

1. *A simple overdraft or loan facility* from his domestic clearing bank. It is both the cheapest and the most flexible facility and may, under certain circumstances be eligible for tax relief. It will usually have to be secured against some collateral.
2. *A foreign-currency, fixed-period loan* to enable him to settle specific transactions in a non-sterling currency. The loan would have to be repaid on the agreed date in the currency nominated, regardless of default or political events or restrictions which occur after the loan is agreed. Certain specialist insurance facilities are available to cover such contingencies but these will add to the cost and should be discussed fully with the lending bank.

3. *Produce loans* for periods of up to three months, which enable importers to bring in large stocks of seasonal products as bulk imports for more detailed distribution. The bank will normally insist on taking title to the goods as security and may require evidence of a firm contract of sale together with adequate insurance of any risk involved. The rate of interest charged for this facility is normally in line with that of an overdraft.
4. *Acceptance credit finance* which is, in effect, a means of discounting bills of exchange through a third party over longer periods than a normal bill (*see* section 5.1.4).
5. *Leasing arrangements*, which are particularly useful as an alternative to outright purchase in the case of capital equipment. The goods are purchased by the leasor and leased to the importing leasee at a rental which recovers the capital cost and interest over a period of around three years. The importing leasee can offset the rental payments against tax. Once the original cost and interest has been recovered, the rental normally continues at a nominal rent during the life of the goods.
6. *Factoring*, which is a means of improving an importer's cash flow by 'selling' his customers' debt to a finance house. For an importer, a factoring service provides the following:
   a. The despatch of invoices to debtors on advice of despatch of goods by the importer.
   b. The collection of money due.
   c. The maintenance of the importer's sales ledger.
   d. The facility to draw between 70 and 80 per cent of outstanding debts immediately they are invoiced out.
   e. The progress chasing of overdue accounts and bad debts.

To make the facility sufficiently attractive to the factor, an importer needs a turnover of something in excess of £100,000 a year.

There are three forms of factoring:
   a. Recourse factoring, which offers the full range of services listed above.
   b. Non-recourse factoring, which offers the same range of facilities as above but, in addition, provides credit insurance and credit status checking before the debts are incurred. This provides a high level of security for both sides but could result in embarrassment if a customer is rejected after negotiations have taken place.
   c. Confidential invoice discounting, where debts are discounted without the provision of any of the other services. The importer maintains his own sales ledger and sends out his own invoices. This can be a useful facility if the importer wishes to conceal the fact that he is using factoring facilities.

The charge or 'discount rate' for factoring services varies considerably according to the risks involved. As a guide, money is advanced ahead of customer payment at a rate of interest of around 1½ per cent above bank rate, and there is an administration fee of 1 to 3 per cent of factored turnover.

An importer can obtain information about all these facilities from his bank or trade association but, manifestly, any advice given will be angled towards the facilities which the informant is able to provide.

An alternative source of finance to the local clearing bank could be one of the trade finance houses, which are modern mutations of the old colonial confirming houses. These, because of their former colonial connections, tend to specialise in particular geographical areas. They normally seek to secure their loans against 'business performance', as evidenced by a viable sales ledger, rather than the more conventional security demanded by clearing banks. Information concerning trade finance houses can be obtained from chambers of commerce or trade associations (and in particular the British Importers Confederation).

7.2.2 Currency arrangements

Manifestly the most important aspects of an imported price is that it should be right (i.e. competitive) and that it should be stable during the period it is on offer to domestic customers. In today's climate of rapidly fluctuating exchange rates, stability is often the harder of the two to achieve.

Payment in sterling obviously produces the most stable situation (although, if the rate goes against sterling, then an importer could find himself operating at a competitive disadvantage to an importer who is operating in another more favourable currency).

Sometimes, trading partners cannot agree to settle in either of their currencies and opt to do business in a third neutral currency. The US dollar is today the most popular of the neutral currencies, even when it comes under severe economic pressure, although both the yen and the Deutschmark are increasingly used in this way. Trading in currencies other than sterling obliges an importer to secure sufficient of that currency at the time it is needed.

There are two ways of purchasing foreign currency: at the prevailing 'spot' price or, at a 'forward' price timed to coincide with the date of liability.

Buying 'spot' means buying your currency needs at a particular point in time at the then current rate – immediately, near the time of settlement or at any date in between when the exchange rate appears to be at its most favourable. In 'spot' trading, the currency is purchased at the prevailing price on that day, for delivery in two days' time.

Buying 'forward' means buying currency for delivery at a specific date in the future at a price agreed today which may be at a premium or discount to the current price, dependent upon the view the market is taking on future prospects.

These spot and forward rates are published daily in the financial press. Importers can also cover their exchange risks in three other ways:

1. By entering into foreign exchange contracts.
2. By making foreign currency deposits.
3. By operating a foreign currency account.

Foreign exchange contracts secure fixed sums of a foreign currency on a fixed date. Such a contract may be a firm undertaking to buy, or be in the form of an option to purchase. Under this system, an importer knows his exact sterling commitment that he will have to meet to settle his foreign currency transaction. Banks will make such contracts up to a year ahead and, in the main trading currencies such as the US dollar, for even longer periods.

A foreign currency deposit account is a convenient way of using any surplus funds to secure foreign currency at today's spot price. By placing the foreign currency on deposit, it earns interest until it needs to be withdrawn to meet obligations.

A foreign currency account is particularly useful to an importer if he is also receiving money in the same currency as his import transactions, because he can avoid the handling cost of individual exchange transactions which may otherwise be heavier than the interest which can be earned on a foreign currency deposit account.

Again, the local clearing bank is usually only too willing to offer advice and assistance in exploring these facilities. If, however, foreign currency transactions are substantial, an importer would be well advised to consult an international bank which specialises in operating currency risk 'hedging' strategies.

8

NEW TECHNOLOGY AND INTERNATIONAL TRADE

Relatively speaking, the application of new technology to importing is still in its infancy. Since the Second World War, the main developments have been containerisation and container handling; communication technology; and computerisation.

Containerisation and container handling have evolved from the application of relatively simple modular engineering techniques which have nonetheless resulted in an enormous increase in flexibility, particularly at terminals when goods are transferred from one distribution system to another, say from rail to road. It has also increased the speed of goods handling, particularly by means of custom-built lifting machinery which is now available at container base points of entry. Containers are now constructed to standard sizes and specifications which make it easy to stack, handle and load them, either directly on to ships or on to lorries for roll-on-roll-off operations. This standardisation now extends to airfreight handling. The organisation of consolidated loads based on standard containers by freight forwarding agents has significantly reduced the freighting charges on small consignments (*see* section 3.5.2).

Communication technology has been applied principally in the form of the widespread use of cable-based telex networks. Telex itself is now more than 50 years old, yet it still holds the dominant position in telecommunications. It is relatively cheap, provides a written confirmation of any transactions or arrangements made through it and is a relatively easy solution to language barriers. It can be used if necessary to hold two-way conversations the content of which is recorded on the printer output. The International Telex Service provides instant communication between some 200 countries throughout the world. The major development since the war has been the terminals themselves which need no longer be simple and rather noisy typewriters. Instead they can provide correctable video screen displays of what is to be transmitted, and sophisticated answering and memorising facilities when there are time lags between business hours in different parts of the world. They can be used to place, acknowledge and progress orders, confirm delivery dates and chase outstanding payments. They can be programmed to transmit to multi-destinations simultaneously and to list and memorise frequently-used addresses in the form of four-letter codes.

The three latest developments are the connection of cable networks to orbiting satellite facilities, the availability of copying machines which are able to transmit facsimiles of documents including official stamps and signatures (which are increasingly being accepted by customs authorities as temporary documents) and the inclusion of telex facilities on intelligent computer terminals (*see* below).

Computers are already in extensive use by the customs services of most advanced countries. They are used mainly to process entries and produce clearance documents and for statistical compilation (*see* section 6.4.11) On account of the mass of data which has to be processed, the systems require large mainframe centrally-located computers which are capable of being fed and interrogated by a network of terminals located at points of entry, importers' premises and other customs locations. The main problem which hinders the worldwide exchange of information held by these computers is the incompatibility not only of the different mainframe computers in use but also of the software (that is to say the programs of instruction which control the processing of data). Much work has still to be done to develop satisfactory interfaces between the main systems. Nor is the activity of the local terminals confined to feeding and interrogating the mainframe computer. Today's intelligent terminals are microcomputers in their own right capable of acting as word processors to replace typewriters and double as telex machines. They can be linked by ordinary telephone lines (through machines known as modems) to other information networks such as Prestel, provide electronic mail facilities and run a wide range of standard, user-friendly programs such as spreadsheets, accounting packages and sophisticated database filing systems. 'Customs 88' (*see* section 6.2) has been introduced primarily to encourage the expansion of computer applications so as to simplify and improve the clearance transactions which are at the heart of international trade.

9

SOURCES OF INFORMATION AND ASSISTANCE

9.1 INSTITUTIONAL FACILITIES

No importer need be short of information and help in what can often be a complex operation fraught with dangers for the unwary and uninformed.

HM Customs and Excise will always be the prime source of objective information about importing into the United Kingdom. Properly conducted import operations give them less trouble so they are always willing to discuss any problems on a 'what if?' basis. However they are not prepared to act as an importer's administrative manager or, for example, do the work of tariff classification and the calculation of tariff valuations which are the responsibility of the importer himself. Local customs houses should always be the first resort for advice, but the addresses for specialist advice have been given earlier in the book in the relevant sections.

The Department of Trade and Industry can issue general guidance on trade regimes, quota systems and legislation which may be pending, particularly in the European Community, but are not concerned with the day-to-day operations of import control and clearance. Again the addresses for specialist advice are given earlier in the book under the relevant sections.

Chambers of commerce have extensive libraries many with sections devoted to international trade, but their expert knowledge of import regimes and problems will depend to a large extent on how involved their members are in external trade. A number of chambers which are close to entry points, such as, for example the Merseyside Chamber of Commerce, are highly expert in this specialist field, and are always glad to help members of other chambers with less expertise if asked.

The British Importers Confederation (BIC) is the major private source of information about import affairs. It exists to represent the interests of importing members on the international scene at all levels and is perhaps the most fruitful source of advice as opposed to information. It has three levels of membership as follows:

1. Ordinary, for importing companies and individual traders.

2. Association, for UK trade associations and similar organisations.
3. International, for foreign organisations engaged in trading in or with the United Kingdom.

It works in close association with the London Chamber of Commerce.

If an importer is not a member through his trade association or chamber of commerce, then individual membership is well worthwhile. Its address is: **The British Importers Confederation**, 69 Cannon Street, London EC4N 5AB (telephone: 01 248 4444).

The Confederation of British Industry (CBI) maintains a lively and wide-ranging interest in international trade, particularly at the representational level, but naturally specialises in exporting. Its headquarters is at Centre Point in London, but it maintains a number of regional offices, which should be the first point of contact. It has particularly close connections with the International Chamber of Commerce.

The International Chamber of Commerce (ICC) has its main offices in Paris and concentrates on issues of international trade in terms of both representing members' interests and of disseminating information. It specialises in spearheading attempts to simplify, rationalise and codify trading practices at the international level. Individual importers who are members of chambers of commerce, trade associations, the CBI or the BIC will usually find that they have indirect access to their facilities and publications. Its address is **The International Chamber of Commerce**, 38 Cours Albert 1er, 75008 Paris, France. It also maintains a branch in the UK in the offices of the CBI at Centre Point, London.

Clearing banks maintain special international sections which analyse trade and are naturally particularly strong in trade finance issues. They are also well informed about trade administration and clearance procedures, as many of their financial packages are dependent on them. The first point of contact should be the local branch manager who will either obtain specialist advice or put the importer in touch directly with a specialist adviser. However, inevitably, the advice which an importer will receive will be slanted towards the facilities which the bank can offer to him, even when more appropriate facilities may be available from other sources.

Trading Standards offices are always prepared to offer advice about the technical aspects of merchandise which an importer may wish to offer for sale in the United Kingdom (*see* section 5.2.6).

Consulates of exporting countries are often as alert and active in support of their exporting industries as are British consulates abroad. They are usually eager to provide advice and information, particularly about possible sources of supply, and to help with export procedures and with commercial visits to their countries.

9.2 USEFUL PUBLICATIONS

The Integrated Tariff of the United Kingdom ('The Tariff') which is published annually is the importer's bible. It sets out in great detail all aspects of duties, levies, tariffs, preferences, merchandise classification, documentation and procedures to be followed. It has already been described in detail in section 6.1.3 and 6.2. It can be obtained from any of HM Stationery Offices.

British Business is a weekly publication by the Department of Trade and Industry. It contains digests of trade statistics, lists, summaries and comments on Customs Notices and, in 'Notices to Importers', provides up-to-date information about trade legislation both domestic and European. It also runs occasional in-depth articles which are, in general, but not always, export-orientated.

Importing Quarterly is published by the British Importers Confederation. It contains, besides general import information and news items, in-depth articles on all specialist aspects of importing, such as finance, insurance, freight handling and, in particular, comments on forthcoming legislation which might affect importers.

The Official Journal of the European Community publishes the full text of all European directives, regulations and decisions about every aspect of Community activity. It is a weighty volume, with much which is not relevant to trade. Its substance is usually available in summary form in *British Business*.

Croner's Reference Book for Importers is a meticulously detailed work of reference on all aspects of import procedures, administration and documentation. It is provided in looseleaf format. Once purchased, it is kept up-to-date with a monthly update or page reprint service available on annual subscription. If *The Tariff* is the importer's bible, then Croner is his Book of Common Prayer. It can be obtained from **Croner's Publications Ltd**, 173 Kingston Road, New Malden, Surrey KT3 3SS.

APPENDIX A   THE TERMS OF TRADE

The International Chamber of Commerce (ICC) has produced a *Guide to Incoterms No. 354* which explains in detail the different 'terms of trade'. The Guide provides full explanations of the various 'shorthand' terms used in international trade to describe the division of responsibilities between supplier, carrier and importer during the process of transferring the goods between the overseas factory and the importer's nominated premises. It can be obtained from ICC Publications SA, 38 Cours Albert 1er, 75008 Paris, France, but most Chambers of Commerce will hold a library copy of the Guide.

A summary of the responsibilities of the overseas supplier in relation to these terms is as follows:

Term	Abbreviation	Responsibilities of foreign vendor
ex Works	ex Works	To have goods available packed or unpacked at works.
Free on Rail/ Free on Transport	FOR/FOT	To provide necessary documentation and bear cost and risk until goods are loaded on rail or transporter.
Free Alongside Ship	FAS	To provide necessary documentation and bear cost and risk until goods are delivered to quay or lighter at port of exit for nominated vessel.
Free on Board	FOB	To provide necessary documentation and bear cost and risk until goods pass ship's rail at exit port. (NB. check terms carefully because other countries have different interpretations).
Free on Aircraft	FOB Aircraft	To provide necessary documentation and bear cost and risk until goods are loaded at named airport.
Free Carrier	Free Carrier	To provide necessary documentation and bear cost and risk until goods are collected by or delivered to the carrier.
Cost and Freight paid to	C&F	To provide necessary documentation and bear all costs including transportation until goods pass the ship's rail at port of entry but not insurance risks.
Cost and Freight	C&F paid to...	As for C&F but delivered to address nominated by importer.

APPENDIX A

Cost, Insurance and Freight	CIF	As for C&F but to include insurance of all risks.
Freight, Insurance and Carriage paid to	FIC paid to...	As for 'F&C paid to . . .' but including insurance for all risks.
ex Ship	ex Ship	To provide necessary documentation and bear all costs and risks of making goods available to importer on board ship.
ex Quay	ex Quay	To provide necessary documentation and bear all costs and risks until goods are delivered to importer or his agent at arrival quayside.
Delivered Frontier	DFrontier	To provide necessary documentation and bear all costs and risks until goods are delivered to importer's representative at a specific customs point *en route* agreed by importer (with importer responsible for clearance and onward documentation).
Delivered Duty Paid	DDP or FRANCO	To provide necessary documentation and bear costs and risks, provide customs clearance and pay duty at point of entry. 'Franco Domicile' means delivered to an address specified by importer. 'Franco Free' means delivered to a freeport.

APPENDIX B INLAND CLEARANCE CENTRES

INLAND CLEARANCE DEPOTS AND INLAND RAIL DEPOTS

Barking Containerbase, Box Lane, Barking	LBL
Barking Containerway, International Freight Terminal, Ripple Road, Barking, Essex	LBR
Birmingham Containerbase, Perry Bar, Birmingham	BPB
Birmingham Inland Rail Depot, Landor Street, Birmingham	BRD
Bristol Inland Clearance Depot, Avonmouth	BSL
Coatbridge Containerbase, Coatbridge, Glasgow	COA
Dagenham Storage Co. Ltd, Dagenham, Essex	LDR
East Anglian Freight Terminal Ltd, Felixstowe	FBE
Erith Inland Clearance Depot, Erith, Kent	EWS
Glasgow Inland Rail Depot, Salkeld Street, Glasgow	GGA
Greenford Inland Clearance Depot, Greenford, Middlesex	LGR
Hull Euroscan Ltd, Dairycoates, Hull	HUD
Leeds Containerbase, Stourton, Leeds	LWR
Speke Freight Terminal, Liverpool	LGA
Liverpool Container Base (Bootle)	BOO
London (East) Inland Clearance Depot, Chobham Farm, Leyton Road, London E15	LCB
London (Stratford) International Freight, London E15	LST
Lenham Inland Clearance Depot, Lenham, Nr. Maidstone	LEN
Manchester Containerbase, Urmston, Lancs.	MBA
Manchester International Freight Terminal, Trafford Park	MIF
Milton Inland Clearance Depot, Milton Trading Estate, Abingdon, Berks	MTN
Northampton Inland Clearance Depot, Round Spinney, Northampton	NRS
Paddock Wood Inland Clearance Depot, Tonbridge, Kent	PWT
Sheepy Park Depot, Renfrew	RSP
Sutton International Freight Terminal, Sutton-in-Ashfield, Notts.	HSA
All other approved depots not listed above	OAD

APPENDIX B

FREE ZONES

Belfast Airport Free Zone	FZT
Birmingham Airport Free Zone	FZM
Cardiff Free Zone	FZF
Liverpool Free Zone	FZL
Prestwick Airport Free Zone	FZK
Southampton Free Zone	FZN

APPENDIX C   THE INTEGRATED TARIFF OF THE UNITED KINGDOM – SPECIMEN PAGE

APPENDIX C

	Commodity codes* 2A plus 2B:		Specific Provisions**	Unit(s) of Quantity	Full rate of Duty – Non-EC Countries	Preferential rates (KEY: see below) Accession rates – Portugal (PT), Spain (ES)	VAT rate
Heading number and description	2A: Intra-EC Imports and ALL Exports	2B: Imports from Non-EC Countries					
1	2A	2B	3	4	5	6	7
48 11 PAPER, PAPERBOARD, CELLULOSE WADDING, AND WEBS OF CELLULOSE FIBRES, COATED, IMPREGNATED, COVERED, SURFACE-COLOURED, SURFACE-DECORATED OR PRINTED, IN ROLLS OR SHEETS, OTHER THAN GOODS OF HEADING NO. 48.03, 48.09, 48.10, OR 48.18:							
Tarred, bituminised or asphalted paper and paperboard	481110 00 0	00		Kg	9%	ACP,OCT,EFTA,GSP,MG,MO,CY,FO,IL,MT,TR,YU—Free: PT—xx%; ES—yy%	S
Gummed or adhesive paper and paperboard: Self Adhesive:							
Tape (pressure-sensitive), paper-based (excluding tapes for medical purposes)	481121 00 1	00		Kg	9%	ACP,OCT,EFTA,GSP,MG,MO,CY,FO,IL,MT,TR,YU—Free: PT—xx%; ES—yy%	S
Other	481121 00 9	00		Kg	9%	ACP,OCT,EFTA,GSP,MG,MO,CY,FO,IL,MT,TR,YU—Free: PT—xx%; ES—yy%	S
Other	481129 00 0	00		Kg	9%	ACP,OCT,EFTA,GSP,MG,MO,CY,FO,IL,MT,TR,YU—Free: PT—xx%; ES—yy%	S
Paper and Paperboard coated, impregnated or covered with plastics (excluding adhesives): Bleached, weighing more than 150g/m²:							
Bleached paper impregnated with acrylic resin and coated with polyvinylidene chloride) having a thickness of not less than 200 and not more than 225 micrometres and of a weight per square metre of not less than 165 and not more than 180 grams	481131 00 0	10	S : Free	Kg	8%	ACP,OCT,EFTA,GSP,MG,MO,CY,FO,IL,MT,TR,YU—Free: PT—xx%; ES—yy%	S
Other		90		Kg	8%	ACP,OCT,EFTA,GSP,MG,MO,CY,FO,IL,MT,TR,YU—Free: PT—xx%; ES—yy%	S
Other: Coated with polyalkenes (eg polyethylene, polypropylene): Weighing less than 225 g/m²:							
Kraft	481139 00 1			Kg			S
Other	481139 00 3			Kg			S
Weighing 225 g/m² or more	481139 00 5			Kg			S
Other	481139 00 9			Kg			S
Coloured paper impregnated with acrylic resin and coated with polyvinylidene chlc-ide) having a thickness of not less than 200 and not more than 225 micrometres and of a weight per square metre of not less than 165 and not more than 180 grams		10	S : Free	Kg	9%	ACP,OCT,EFTA,GSP,MG,MO,CY,FO,IL,MT,TR,YU—Free: PT—xx%; ES—yy%	S
Other		90		Kg	9%	ACP,OCT,EFTA,GSP,MG,MO,CY,FO,IL,MT,TR,YU—Free: PT—xx%; ES—yy%	S
Paper and paperboard, coated, impregnated or covered with wax, paraffin wax, stearin, oil or glycerol	481140 00 0	00		Kg	9%	ACP,OCT,EFTA,GSP,MG,MO,CY,FO,IL,MT,TR,YU—Free: PT—xx%; ES—yy%	S
Other paper, paperboard, cellulose wadding and webs of soft cellulose	481190 00 0	00		Kg	9%	ACP,OCT,EFTA,GSP,MG,MO,CY,FO,IL,MT,TR,YU—Free: PT—xx%; ES—yy%	S

APPENDIX D   THE SINGLE ADMINISTRATIVE DOCUMENT (C88) – SPECIMEN FORM

APPENDIX D

> THIS SET OF FORMS IS PRINTED ON NCR PAPER. IF COMPLETING BY HAND, WRITE IN BLOCK LETTERS, USING A BALLPOINT PEN AND APPLY MAXIMUM PRESSURE WITH THE SET RESTING ON A FIRM SURFACE.

HANDLE WITH CARE

EUROPEAN COMMUNITY

A OFFICE OF DISPATCH/EXPORT

1 | **2** Consignor/Exporter No

I DECLARATION

3 Forms | **4** Loading lists

5 Items | **6** Total packages | **7** Reference number

Copy for the country of dispatch/export

8 Consignee No

9 Person responsible for financial settlement No

10 Country first destin | **11** Trading country | **13** CAP

14 Declarant/Representative No

15 Country of dispatch/export | **15** C disp./exp. Code | **17** Country destin Code

16 Country of origin | **17** Country of destination

18 Identity and nationality of means of transport at departure | **19** Ctr | **20** Delivery terms

21 Identity and nationality of active means of transport crossing the border | **22** Currency and total amount invoiced | **23** Exchange rate | **24** Nature of transaction

25 Mode of transport at the border | **26** Inland mode of transport | **27** Place of loading | **28** Financial and banking data

1 | **29** Office of exit | **30** Location of goods

31 Packages and description of goods | Marks and numbers — Container No(s) — Number and kind | **32** Item No | **33** Commodity Code

34 Country origin Code | **35** Gross mass (kg)

37 PROCEDURE | **38** Net mass (kg) | **39** Quota

40 Summary declaration/Previous document

41 Supplementary units

44 Additional information/ Documents produced/ Certificates and authorisations

A I Code

46 Statistical value

47 Calculation of taxes | Type | Tax base | Rate | Amount | MP | **48** Deferred payment | **49** Identification of warehouse

B ACCOUNTING DETAILS

Total

50 Principal No | Signature | **C** OFFICE OF DEPARTURE

51 Intended offices of transit (and country) | represented by Place and date

52 Guarantee not valid for | Code | **53** Office of destination (and country)

D CONTROL BY OFFICE OF DEPARTURE Result Seals affixed Number identity Time limit (date) Signature

Stamp

54 Place and date

Signature and name of declarant/representative

APPENDIX E LIST OF FORMS REPLACED BY THE SAD (C88)

Form No.	Title
C10	General Import Entry.
C11	Customs Import Entry (Trader Input).
C12	Customs Import Entry (Customs Input).
C15	Customs Import Entry (Abbreviated).
C31	Eire Export/UK Import Declaration for Community Goods – Irish Land Boundary.
C32	Export UK/Import Eire Declaration for Community Goods – Irish Land Boundary.
C60	Goods exported from Customs Warehouse.
C63	Export declaration for HCO ex bonded warehouse and goods on which Returned Goods Relief may be claimed.
C63A	Export declaration for goods subject to export licences.
C91	Entry for goods imported under the Period Entry (Imports) Scheme.
C170	Postal Import Entry.
C271	Export Pre-Shipment Advice.
C273	Export Declaration.
C295	Export Declaration for CAP goods.
C295A	Entry for IBAP Schedulers on ex Works Sales
C1126	T2L Community Status Document.
C1138	T Form. Full Community Transit.
C1334	Export Declaration for Inward Processing Relief goods.
C1337	Export Declaration: Certificate of Shipment for repayment claims.
C&E596	Export Declaration for beer exported on drawback.
C&E1172	Export Declaration for goods on which repayment of Customs Duty, etc. is claimed and for goods for which temporary importation has been allowed.
C&E1173	Export Declaration for Goods for Outward Processing/Standard Exchange Relief.

Form No.	Title
EX 115	Export Declaration for Tinctures or Spirits of Wine exported on drawback.
HO59	Export Declaration for HCO goods including composite goods at fixed rates exported on drawback.
W60	Export Declaration for Wet Goods and Tobacco Products exported from Bonded Warehouse.
TP9	Export Declaration for tobacco products ex registered premises exported without payment of duty.
TP 10	Tobacco Products – Export Declaration or Certificate of Destination and claim for Credit/Repayment of Duty.

APPENDIX F THE INTERNATIONAL TRADING AFFILIATION NETWORK

Country	State of development	OECD	GATT	EEC relationship	EEC GSP	MFA	FTA member	OPEC
(1)	(2)	(3)	(4)	(5)	(6)	(7)	(8)	(9)
Afghanistan	LDDC				GSP			
Albania	STN							
Algeria	LDC		GATT	MA	GSP			OPEC
Angola	LDC		GATT	ACP	GSP			
Anguilla	LDC			OCT				
Antigua	LDC		GATT	ACP	GSP		CARICOM	
Antilles	LDC			OCT	GSP			
Argentina	NIC		GATT	PA	GSP	MFA	LAFTA	
Aruba	LDC			OCT	GSP			
Ascension	LDC			OCT				
Australia	FIC	OECD	GATT					
Austria	FIC	OECD	GATT			MFA	EFTA	
Bahamas	LDC		GATT	ACP	GSP		CARICOM	
Bahrain	LDC		GATT		GSP			
Bangladesh	LLDC		GATT	PA	GSP	MFA		
Barbados	LDC		GATT	ACP	GSP		CARICOM	
Belgium	FIC	OECD	GATT	EEC		MFA		
Belize	LDC		GATT	ACP	GSP		CARICOM	
Benin	LDDC		GATT	ACP				
Birkina Fasso	LDDC			ACP	GSP			
Bolivia	LDC				GSP	MFA	LAFTA	
Bonaire	LDC			OCT	GSP			
Botswana	LDDC		GATT	ACP	GSP			
Brazil	NIC		GATT	PA	GSP	MFA	LAFTA	
Brit. Antarctic Terr.	LDC			OCT				
Brit. Ind. Ocean Terr.	LDC			OCT				
British Virgin Isl.	LDC			OCT				
Brunei	LDC			OCT			ASEAN	
Bulgaria	STN					MFA	COMECON	
Burma	LDC		GATT		GSP			
Burundi	LDDC		GATT	ACP				
Cameroon	LDC		GATT	ACP	GSP			
Canada	FIC	G7	GATT			MFA		
Cape Verde	LDDC		GATT	ACP	GSP			
Cayman Islands	LDC			OCT				
Cen. African Rep.	LDDC		GATT	ACP				
Chad	LDDC		GATT	ACP				
Chile	NIC		GATT		GSP	MFA	LAFTA	

APPENDIX F

Country (1)	State of development (2)	OECD (3)	GATT (4)	EEC relationship (5)	EEC GSP (6)	MFA (7)	FTA member (8)	OPEC (9)
China (Rep. of)	STN				GSP	MFA		
Colombia	NIC		GATT		GSP	MFA	LAFTA	
Comoros	LDDC			ACP				
Congo	LDC		GATT	ACP	GSP			
Costa Rica	NIC				GSP	MFA	ODECA	
Cuba	LDC		GATT		GSP			
Curacao	LDC		GATT		GSP			
Cyprus	LDC		GATT	MA	GSP			
Czechoslovakia	STN					MFA	COMECON	
Denmark	FIC	OECD	GATT	EEC		MFA		
Djibuti	LDC			ACP				
Dominica	LDC		GATT	ACP		MFA	CARICOM	
Dominican Republic	LDC		GATT		GSP			
Ecuador	NIC				GSP	MFA	LAFTA	OPEC
Egypt	LDC		GATT	MA	GSP	MFA		
El Salvador	LDC				GSP	MFA	ODECA	
Equatorial Guinea	LDDC		GATT	ACP				
Ethiopia	LDDC			ACP	GSP			
Falkland Isles	LDC			OCT				
Fiji	LDC		GATT	ACP	GSP			
Finland	FIC	OECD	GATT			MFA	EFTA	
France	FIC	G5	GATT	EEC		MFA		
Gabon	LDC		GATT	ACP	GSP			OPEC
Gambia	LDDC		GATT	ACP				
German Dem. Republic	STN						COMECON	
German Fed. Republic	FIC	G5	GATT	EEC		MFA		
Ghana	LDC		GATT	ACP	GSP			
Greece	FIC	OECD	GATT	EEC		MFA		
Gibraltar	LDC		GATT	OCT	GSP			
Greenland	LDC			OCT	GSP			
Grenada	LDC		GATT	ACP	GSP		CARICOM	
Guam	LDC				GSP			
Guatemala	LDC				GSP	MFA	ODECA	
Guinea	LDDC			ACP	GSP			
Guinea Bissau	LDDC		GATT	ACP	GSP			
Guyana	LDC		GATT	ACP	GSP		CARICOM	
Haiti	LDDC		GATT		GSP	MFA		
Honduras	LDC		GATT		GSP	MFA	ODECA	
Hungary	STN		GATT				COMECON	
Hong Kong	NIC		GATT	OCT	GSP	MFA		
Iceland	FIC	OECD	GATT				EFTA	
India	LDC		GATT	PA	GSP	MFA		
Indonesia	LDC		GATT		GSP	MFA	ASEAN	OPEC
Iran	LDC				GSP			OPEC
Iraq	LDC				GSP			OPEC
Ireland	FIC	ODEC	GATT	EEC		MFA		
Israel	NIC		GATT	MA		MFA		
Italy	FIC	G7	GATT	EEC		MFA		
Ivory Coast	LDC		GATT	ACP	GSP			
Jamaica	LDC		GATT	ACP	GSP		CARICOM	
Japan	FIC	G5	GATT					
Jordan	LDC			PA				
Kampuchea	LDC		GATT					
Kenya	LDC		GATT	ACP	GSP			

APPENDIX F

Country	State of development	OECD	GATT	EEC relationship	EEC GSP	MFA	FTA member	OPEC
(1)	(2)	(3)	(4)	(5)	(6)	(7)	(8)	(9)
Kiribati	LDC		GATT	ACP				
Korea, North	STN							
Korea, South	NIC		GATT		GSP	MFA		
Kuwait	LDC		GATT		GSP			OPEC
Laos	LDDC							
Lebanon	LDC			PA	GSP			
Lesotho	LDDC		GATT	ACP	GSP			
Liberia	LDDC			ACP	GSP			
Libya	LDC				GSP			OPEC
Liechtenstein	FIC						EFTA	
Luxembourg	FIC	OECD	GATT	EEC		MFA		
Macao	LDC			OTC	GSP	MFA		
Madagascar	LDC		GATT	ACP				
Malawi	LDDC			ACP	GSP			
Malaysia	NIC		GATT		GSP	MFA	ASEAN	
Maldives	LDDC		GATT		GSP			
Mali	LDDC		GATT	ACP				
Malta	LDC		GATT	MA				
Mauritania	LDC		GATT	ACP				
Mauritius	LDC		GATT	ACP	GSP			
Mayotte	LDC			OCT				
Mexico	NIC		GATT	PA	GSP	MFA	LAFTA	
Montserrat	LDC			OCT			CARICOM	
Morocco	LDC		GATT	ACP	GSP			
Mozambique	LDC		GATT	ACP	GSP			
Nepal	LDDC				GSP			
Netherlands	FIC	OECD	GATT	EEC		MFA		
Netherlands Antilles	LDC			OCT	GSP			
New Caledonia	LDC			OCT				
New Zealand	FIC	OECD	GATT					
Nicaragua	LDC		GATT		GSP			
Niger	LDDC		GATT	ACP				
Nigeria	LDC		GATT	ACP	GSP			OPEC
Norway	FIC	OECD	GATT				EFTA	
Oman	LDC		GATT		GSP			
Pakistan	LDC		GATT	PA	GSP	MFA		
Panama	LDC				GSP			
Papua New Guinea	LDC		GATT	ACP	GSP			
Paraguay	LDC				GSP		LAFTA	
Peru	LDC		GATT		GSP	MFA		
Philippines	LDC		GATT		GSP	MFA	ASEAN	
Pitcairn	LDC			OCT				
Poland	STN					MFA	COMECON	
Portugal	FIC	OECD	GATT	EEC		MFA		
Qatar	LDC		GATT		GSP			OPEC
Romania	STN		GATT		GSP	MFA	COMECON	
Rwanda	LDDC		GATT	ACP				
St Christopher & Nevis	LDC			ACP			CARICOM	
St Helena	LDC			OCT				
St Lucia	LDC		GATT	ACP			CARICOM	
St Pierre & Miquelon	LDC			OCT				
St Vincent	LDC		GATT	ACP			CARICOM	
Samoa, Western	LDDC			ACP	GSP			
Sao Tome & Principe	LDDC			ACP	GSP			

APPENDIX F

Country (1)	State of development (2)	OECD (3)	GATT (4)	EEC relationship (5)	EEC GSP (6)	MFA (7)	FTA member (8)	OPEC (9)
Saudi Arabia	LDC				GSP			OPEC
Senegal	LDC		GATT	ACP	GSP			
Seychelles	LDDC		GATT	ACP				
Sharjah	LDC				GSP			
Sierra Leone	LDDC		GATT	ACP	GSP			
Singapore	NIC		GATT		GSP	MFA	ASEAN	
Solomon Islands	LDC		GATT	ACP	GSP			
Somalia	LDDC			ACP				
South Africa	FIC		GATT					
S. Georgia & Sandwich I.	LDC			OCT				
Spain	FIC	OECD	GATT	EEC		MFA		
Sri Lanka	LDC		GATT	PA	GSP	MFA		
Sudan	LDDC			ACP	GSP			
Surinam	LDC		GATT	ACP	GSP			
Swaziland	LDC		GATT	ACP	GSP			
Sweden	FIC	OECD	GATT			MFA	EFTA	
Switzerland	FIC	OECD	GATT			MFA	EFTA	
Syria	LDC			PA	GSP			
Taiwan	NIC					MFA		
Tanzania	LDDC		GATT	ACP	GSP			
Thailand	LDC		GATT		GSP	MFA	ASEAN	
Togo	LDDC		GATT	ACP	GSP			
Tonga	LDDC		GATT	ACP	GSP			
Trinidad & Tobago	LDC		GATT	ACP	GSP		CARICOM	
Tunalu	LDC		GATT	ACP				
Tunisia	LDC		GATT	MA	GSP			
Turkey	NIC	OECD	GATT	MA		MFA		
Turks & Caicos I.	LDC			OCT				
UAE	LDC		GATT					OPEC
Uganda	LDDC		GATT	ACP				
United Kingdom	FIC	G5	GATT	EEC		MFA		
Upper Volta	LDC		GATT					
Uruguay	NIC		GATT	PA	GSP	MFA	LAFTA	
USA	FIC	G5	GATT			MFA		
USSR	STN						COMECON	
Vanautu	LDC			ACP				
Venezuela	NIC				GSP		LAFTA	OPEC
Vietnam	LDC				GSP			
Wallis & Hoorn	LDC			OCT				
Yemen, North	LDDC		GATT		GSP			
Yemen, South	LDDC				GSP			
Yugoslavia	NIC	OECD	GATT	PA	GSP	MFA		
Zaire	LDC		GATT	ACP				
Zambia	LDC		GATT	ACP				
Zimbabwe	LDC		GATT	ACP	GSP			

This appendix is a tabulation of the network of trading relationships described in detail in sections 1.2, 3.1, 3.2 and 4.2. The initials in the tabulation translate as follows:

Column 2 – State of development
See section 3.1.2.

FIC – Fully industrialised countries. (Rich.)
NIC – Newly industrialised countries. (Becoming rich.)

APPENDIX F

LDC   – Less developed countries. (Poor.)
LDDC – Less developed developing countries. (Poorest of the poor.)
STN   – State trading nations. (Wealth cannot be measured in the same way.)

Column 3 – Membership of the Organisation of Economic Co-operation and Development (OECD)
See section 3.1.4.

OECD – Membership of OECD. This is known as 'the rich man's club'. Within it there are two even more exclusive clubs:

G5   – The Group of 5 (USA, UK, Japan, Germany and France).
G7   – The Group of 7 (G5 plus Italy and Canada).

Column 4 – Membership of the General Agreement on Tariffs and Trade (GATT)
See section 1.2.4.

Column 5 – Other countries' relationship with the European Community
See section 3.2.1.

EEC – Full Community member.
MA – Signatory of a Mediterranean Associate Agreement.
PA   – Signatory of a Trade Preference Agreement.
ACP – African, Caribbean or Pacific Associate (Lome Convention Signatory). Former dependencies of member states who are now independent countries.
OCT – Overseas Countries and Territories who are still dependencies of member states.

Column 6 – Beneficiaries of the EEC generalised scheme of preferences (GSP)
See section 3.1.6.

Column 7 – Signatories of the Multi-Fibre Arrangement (MFA)
See section 4.2.4.

Column 8 – Membership of other free trade and Common Market organisations
See section 3.1.

COMECON – Council for Mutual Economic Assistance.
EFTA   – European Free Trade Association.
LAFTA   – Latin American Free Trade Association.
ODECA   – Central American Common Market.
CARICOM – Caribbean Common Market.

Column 9 – Membership of the Organisation of Petroleum Exporting Countries (OPEC)
See section 1.2.1.

INDEX

A Manager's Guide to International Road Freighting, 108
ad valorem valuation, 126
African, Caribbean and Pacific states *see* EEC, Lomé Convention
aftersales servicing, 81
Agricultural Levies (Outward Processing Relief) Order of 1976, 40, 123
agricultural support schemes, 67–8
 subsidy schemes, 67
 deficiency payment schemes, 67
 intervention schemes, 68
Alaska, 10
Albania, 26
Algeria, 9, 32
Antigua, 29
anti-dumping duties, 117
Argentina, 19, 32, 56
Association of Chambers of Commerce, 101
Association of East Asian Nations (ASEAN), 28, 29
Australia, 29, 56, 92
Austria, 18, 29, 56

Bahamas, 29
Bangladesh, 32, 57
Barbados, 29
barter arrangements, 41
Belfast, 45
Belgium, 8, 15, 30
Belize, 29
Bellport, 116
Bill of Lading Act 1855, 106
bills of exchange, 78
Board of Trade, 22
Bolivia, 29, 57
Brazil, 29, 32, 56
'British Business', 22, 36, 118, 119, 120, 131, 140
British Importers Confederation, 44, 55, 101, 134, 138–9
Brunei, 28

Bulgaria, 25, 57
Business Monitor MQ10, 37
Business Statistics Office, 23
buyback agreements, 41

CADDIA, 101
Canada, 30, 56, 92, 93
Cardiff, 45, 106
Carriage of Goods by Sea Act 1924, 106
Caribbean Common Market (Caricom), 29
Cassis de Dijon case, 62–3, 64
Central American Common Market (ODECA), 29
chambers of commerce, 138
Chatham, 116
Chile, 29
China, Peoples Republic of, 13, 26, 34, 42, 50, 57, 118, 119
Classification, Packaging and Labelling of Dangerous Substances Regulation 1984, 108
clearing banks, 139
Colombia, 29, 56
common customs tariff (CCT), 15, 16
Common Market *see* EEC
communication technology, 136
compensation agreements, 41
computer applications for importing, 137
Confederation of British Industry, 101, 139
consular services, 139
containerisation, 136
consolidation *see* freight handling, groupage
consumer protection, 86–7
 Consumer Protection Act 1987, 113
Copenhagen, 45
Cory Bros Ltd, 109
Costa Rica, 29
Council for Mutual Economic Assistance (COMECON), 13, 18, 25
Council of Europe, 112
counter-trade, 26, 41
countervailing duties, 122

157

cost, insurance and freight (CIF), 35, 121, 130
Croner's Reference Book for Importers, 140
Cuba, 25
currency, 134–5
  buying forward, 135
  buying 'spot', 134
  currency controls, 4, 50
  foreign currency accounts, 135
  foreign exchange contracts, 135
'Customs 88', 94–102, 137
  Classifying your imports, (CDC 100), 102
  correlation tables, 95
  information notes, 98, 99, 101
  liaison officers, 102
  see also Single Administrative Document (SAD)
Customs and Excise Management Act 1979, 128
Customs Consolidation Act 1876, 89
Customs Co-operation Council Nomenclature (CCCN), 93
'Customs Handling of Import and Export Freight' (CHIEF), 94, 100–1
customs import entry system (CIE), 115, 116, 127
Customs Notices, 91
  Notice 121, 132
  Notice 221, 124
  Notice 232, 118
  Notice 235, 39, 82, 123
  Notice 252, 126, 127, 128, 130
  Notice 464, 464A, 105, 116
  Notice 480, 116
  Notice 484, 91, 99, 105, 109, 115, 116, 121, 125
  Notice 750, 750B, 109, 117
  Notice 751, 109
  Notice 753, 109
  Notice 771, 119
  Notice 780, 121, 123
  Notice 781, 121
  Notice 782, 121
  Notice 790, 121
  Notice 826, 119
  Notice 828, 125
  Notice 848, 116
customs removal note (C130), 116
customs valuation, 126–8
  Customs Valuation Branch, 128
Cyprus, 32
Czechoslovakia, 25, 57

Data Interchange in Shipping project, (DISH), 80
Denmark, 18, 30
Department of Trade and Industry (DTI), 22–4, 34, 35, 48, 85, 91, 118, 120, 129, 138

departmental entry processing system (DEPS), 101, 115
Dillon Round, 14
Direct Trader Input (DTI), 101, 115, 116
distribution of total world trade, 35
Domenica, 29, 57
Dover (East and West Docks), 115

Ecuador, 9, 29
Egypt, 32, 50, 56
Eire *see* Ireland
El Salvador, 29, 56
EM leaflets, 122
entrepot trading, 38
European Economic Community (EEC), 8, 15–9, 23, 24, 26, 31, 36, 39, 47, 56, 61–70, 94, 116, 121, 125, 127
  abuse of dominant position, 55, 66
  agricultural levies, 45, 49, 122
  Brussels Tariff Nomenclature (BYN), 93
  Commission, 16, 19, 30, 65, 92
  Common Agricultural Policy (CAP), 30, 36, 49, 51, 62, 67–70, 93, 117, 118, 121
  common community tariff, 61
  common competition policy, 61, 65
  common customs tariff (CCT), 48, 92, 94
  community budget, 67, 68
  community status, 117
  community transit system (CT), 117–8
  Council of Ministers, 16, 34, 49, 65, 68, 112
  Customs Union, 19, 114, 130
  directives, 17, 112
  Economic and Social Committee, 16
  European Assembly, 16
  European Court of Justice, 16, 49, 61, 62, 65, 66, 121
  European currency unit (ECU), 69, 121
  FEOGA, 68
  free circulation, 48, 61
  generalised scheme of preferences (GSP), 33, 119–20
  guarantee fund, 68
  guidance fund, 68
  harmonisation policy, 17, 61, 64
  integrated customs tariff (TARIC), 94, 95, 96–7, 130
  Lomé Convention, 31, 32, 119
  Mediterranean associate agreements, 32, 54, 119
  monetary compensation amounts (MCAs), 62, 69, 121, 122
  negotiating mandates, 28
  regulations, 16
  Treaty of Rome, 15, 52, 55, 62, 67, 117, 120
European Free Trade Association (EFTA), 18, 32, 119, 125

INDEX

excise duties *see* HM Customs and Excise

fax facilities, 137
Felixstowe, 116
Finland, 30, 56
Folkestone docks, 115
France, 8, 15, 17, 30
free on board (FOB), 35
free trade zones, 45–7, 124–5
   free zone input document (FID), 124
   free zone release authority (FRA), 124
   free zone release from warehousing (FRW), 124
   free zone status document (STATDOC), 124
   freight exit document (FED), 125
   out of charge note (C130), 125
freight forwarding agents, 44
   Institute of, 43, 101
freight handling, 103–9
   groupage, 44, 103, 136
   sealed containers and vehicles, 104
   TIR carnets and procedures, 105
Freightliners Ltd, 109
fully-industrialised countries (FICs), 13, 26
Fulton Report, 20

Gabon, 9
Gatwick Airport, 116
General Agreement on Tariffs and Trade (GATT), 8, 13–5, 19, 23, 26, 28, 29, 31, 48, 49, 56–61, 91, 128
   anti-dumping procedures, 53
   derogation from general principles, 53
   most favoured nation principle, 13, 31, 50, 93
   valuation code, 126
   voluntary restraint agreements (VVRAs), 54–5
generalised schemes of preference (GSPs), 31
   EEC scheme, 33–4
Germany, East (German Democratic Republic), 25
Germany, West (German Federal Republic), 8, 15, 17, 30
goods against consignment, 73
goods against order, 73
government subsidies, 51
Great Britain, 6–8, 12, 15, 17, 18, 20, 30, 33, 35, 45, 47, 75, 94
   the structure of UK trade, 35–8
Great Silk Route, 5
Great Yarmouth, 116
Greece, 18, 29, 48, 49, 50, 117
green rate, 69, 121
Grenada, 29
Grimsby, 116
Group of Five, 30

Group of Seven, 30
Guatemala, 29, 56
Guide to Incoterms No 354, 43, 74, 141–2
Guyana, 29

HM Customs and Excise, 21–2, 40, 50, 81, 85, 121, 138
   Bill of Entry Service, 37
   charges, 48
   collections, 90
   customs duties, 6, 131
   entry documentation, 115
   entry procedures, 89–91
   excise duties, 48, 61, 131
   legal instruments, 89
HM Stationery Office, 37, 95
Hague Rules of 1921, 106
Haiti, 56
Hamburg, 45
harmonisation policy *see* European Economic Community
Harmonised Commodity Description and Coding System (HS), 93, 94
Harwich, 116
health and safety, 86–7
   executive, 108
Heathrow Airport, 116
Holland, 8, 15, 30
Honduras, 29
Hong Kong, 14, 39, 45, 56, 57, 60, 61
Hull, 116
Hume, 4
Hungary, 25, 56

Iceland, 18, 29
Immingham, 116
implied warranties, 82
Import Duty (Outward Processing Relief) Regulations of 1976, 40, 123
import finance, 132–4
   acceptance credit finance, 133
   discount rate, 133
   factoring, 133
   fixed period loan in foreign currency, 132
   leasing arrangements, 133
   loan facility, 132
   produce loans, 133
import licence, 90
   Import Licencing Board, 119
   open general import licence (OGIL), 90
   special licence, 90
   surveillance licence, 90
Import of Goods (Control) Order 1954, 89
Importing Quarterly, 140
India, 32, 56
Indonesia, 9, 28, 57
inland clearance centres, 105, 143–4
insurance, 109–14
   floating policies, 110

no fault liability, 111
open policies, 110
Integrated Tariff of the United Kingdom, The, 49, 89, 91, 92, 93, 94, 96, 115, 119, 126, 140
Intercontainer Société Cooperative, 109
International Carriage of Dangerous Goods by Road (ARD), 108
International Carriage of Perishable Foodstuffs Regulation 1985, 108
International Chamber of Commerce (ICC), 43, 74, 76, 77, 80, 139
  Court of Arbitration, 43
International Telex Service, 136
Intervention Board of Agricultural Products (IBAP), 91, 121, 122
intra-trade, 15
invisible trade, 7
inward processing relief, 39, 123
Ipswich, 116
Iran, 9
Iraq, 9
Ireland, 18, 30
Israel, 9, 27, 32, 56
Italy, 15, 17, 30

Jamaica, 29, 56
Japan, 7, 8, 15, 28, 30, 54, 56, 57, 92, 93
Jordan, 32

Kennedy Round, 14
Korea, North, 26
Korea, South, 56, 60
Kuwait, 9, 29

LACES, 101
Latin American Free Trade Area (LAFTA), 29
law of comparative costs, 3
Lebanon, 32
Less Developed Countries (LDCs), 27, 31, 33
Lesser Developed Developing Countries (LDDCs), 27, 34
letters of credit, 79
Libya, 9
linkage agreements, 41
Liverpool, 106, 115
  freeport, 45
Lomé Convention *see* European Economic Community
London Chamber of Commerce, 76
London Court of Arbitrators, 76
London Docks, 115
Luxembourg, 15, 30

Macao, 56, 57, 60
Malaysia, 28, 56
Malta, 32

Manchester Airport, 116
  Docks, 116
Marine Insurance Act 1906, 110
mercantilism, 4
Mexico, 10, 29, 32, 56
Mills, John Stuart, 4
modems, 137
Mongolia, 25
Montserrat, 29
Morocco, 32
most favoured nation principle (MFN) *see* General Agreement on Tariffs and Trade
multi-fibre arrangement (MFA), 33, 50, 55–61, 119, 120–1
  basket extractor mechanism, 59, 129
  bilateral agreements, 57–8
  burden sharing, 62
  market disruption, 57–9
  quotas, 58, 126
  reasonable departure clause, 60

Netherlands *see* Holland
New Zealand, 30, 69, 92
newly-industrialised countries (NICs), 14, 26, 33
Nicaragua, 29, 56, 57
Nigeria, 9
NIMEXE, 94
non-tariff barriers, 4, 51
'Nordic' clause, 58
North Sea oil, 10, 12–3, 36
North-South dialogue, 27
Northcote-Trevelyn Report, 20
Norway, 18, 29, 56, 57

Official Journal of the European Community, 112, 121, 140
oil crises, 1973–8, 8–11
Oman, 29
orderly marketing, 13
orders for new business, 74
  settlement terms and payments, 78
  terms and conditions, 77
Organisation for Economic Co-operation and Development (OCED), 29–31, 34, 130
Organisation of Petroleum Exporting Countries (OPEC), 9–11, 29, 36
outward processing relief (OPR), 39, 123
Overseas Trade Statistics, 35, 130

Pakistan, 32, 56
Paraguay, 29
period entry system, 116, 128
Peru, 57
Philippines, 28, 56
Poland, 25, 56
Poole, 117

Portsmouth, 116
Portugal, 9, 18, 29, 48, 50, 117
President of the Board of Trade, 23
Prestwick Airport, 45
Privy Council, 23
product pricing, 83
  delivered price, 84
  ex-works price, 83
  landed price, 84
  unit manufactured price, 83

Qatar, 9, 29
quotas, 4, 49–50

Ramsgate, 116
Reinheitsgebot edict, 63
requirements of exporting countries, 85
Ricardo, 4
Rochester, 116
Romania, 25, 34, 56
Ro-Ro ferries, 107
Rotterdam, 39, 45
  spot market, 9, 11
rules of origin, 125–6

Sale of Goods Act, 1893 and 1979, 75, 82
samples, 80–1
Saudi Arabia, 9, 11, 29
Schipol Airport, 45
Shannon Airport, 45
Sheerness, 116
shipment by air, 107
shipment by rail, 108
  simplified procedures, 109
shipment by road, 107
shipment by sea, 106
Simplification of International Procedures Board (SITPRO), 80, 101
Singapore, 39, 45, 56, 58
Single Administrative Document (SAD – C88), 91, 97–100, 115, 117
  forms replaced by, 149–50
  specimen form, 146
Smith, Adam, 4, 21
  Institute, 47
specification buying, 77
South Africa, 27, 92
Southampton, 45, 106, 116
Soviet Union, 13, 25
Spain, 6, 18, 30, 48, 50, 56, 57, 117
Sri Lanka, 32, 56
St Kitts-Nevis, 29
St Lucia, 29
St Vincent and the Grenadines, 29
STABEX, 33
Standard Code of Practice on Documentary Credits, 80
state trading nations (STNs), 25, 41, 42
Statistics of Foreign Trade, 34

Strasbourg Convention, 112
subsidies, 4
Supply of Goods (Implied Terms) Act 1973, 82
suspension of duty, 129
Sutton Freight Terminal, 116
Sweden, 18, 30, 56
Switzerland, 18, 45, 56, 58
Syria, 32
SYSMON, 33

Taiwan, 14, 27, 57, 58, 60
Tariff, The, *see* The Integrated Tariff of the UK
tariffs, 4
tariff trade code number (TTCN), 93
Teesport, 116
Telex, 136
Thailand, 28, 57
Tilbury Docks, 115
Tokyo Round, 14
trade statistics, 129
trader unique reference number (TURN), 132
Trades Descriptions Act 1986, 126
trading standards officers, 88, 139
transaction preliminaries, 73–4
treasury, 20, 45
Treaty of Rome *see* European Economic Community
Trinidad and Tobago, 29
Tunisia, 32
Turkey, 30, 32, 56

Uniform Rules for Collection, 80
unit measurement of value, 126
United Arab Emirates, 9, 29
United Kingdom *see* Great Britain
United Kingdom Law Commission, 112
United Nations Conference on Trade and Development, 31
United States of America, 7, 8, 15, 28, 30, 45, 51, 54, 56, 60, 67, 92, 93
Uruguay, 29, 32, 57
  Uruguay Round, 14

Value Added Tax (VAT), 16, 22, 45, 47, 61, 81, 89, 116, 117, 118, 131–2
value build-up sheet (C89), 99, 127
Venezuela, 9, 29
Vienna, 41, 42
Vietnam, 25, 26

Wealth of Nations, The, 21
world wars, 7

Yes Minister, 20
Yugoslavia, 26, 30, 32, 34, 56